350+

KNITTING

*Tips, Techniques,
and Trade Secrets*

350+
KNITTING
Tips, Techniques,
and Trade Secrets

BETTY BARNDEN

ST. MARTIN'S GRIFFIN
NEW YORK

350 + Knitting Tips, Techniques, and
Trade Secrets

A Quarto Book
Copyright © 2007 & 2017 by Quarto Inc.

Library of Congress Cataloging-in-Publication
Data Available Upon Request

ISBN 978-1-250-12512-5

Our books may be purchased in bulk for
promotional, educational, or business use. Please
contact your local bookseller or the Macmillan
Corporate and Premium Sales Department at
1-800-221-7945, extension 5442, or by e-mail at
MacmillanSpecialMarkets@macmillan.com.

First U.S. Edition: July 2017
10 9 8 7 6 5 4 3 2 1

QUAR: KTT2

Conceived, designed, and produced by
Quarto Publishing plc
The Old Brewery
6 Blundell Street, London
N7 9BH
www.quartoknows.com

Project Editor: **Lindsay Kaubi**
Art Editor: **Julie Joubinaux**
Editor and Pattern Checker: **Betsy Hosegood**
Designer: **Jon Wainwright**
Assistant Art Director: **Caroline Guest**
Illustrators: **Kuo Kang Chen**
Photographer: **Phil Wilkins**
Proofreader: **Susan Niner Janes**
Indexer: **Diana LeCore**
Art Director: **Moira Clinch**
Publisher: **Paul Carslake**

Color separation by Cypress Colours (HK) Ltd, Hong Kong
Printed in China by 1010 printing international Ltd.

Contents

Introduction

Knitting is a flexible, adaptable craft, and every knitter develops her (or his) own range of favorite techniques. Over the centuries, many different methods of knitting have been invented in various parts of the world and then passed down and improved upon through the generations. From the delicate lace shawls of the Shetland Isles to the circular techniques used to make the intricate, colorful hats and purses of the Andes, there's always something new for a keen knitter to discover.

Yarns and designs are available from all over the world thanks to the internet, and today's knitters are both inventive and multi-skilled, learning from the traditions of the past and experimenting with new combinations of yarns, stitches, and construction.

Whether you want to follow a printed pattern or create your own designs, there's a bewildering range of yarns, styles, and techniques to choose from. This book includes all the basic information you need to knit with confidence and avoid expensive mistakes.

Beginners start here: Novice knitters should begin by studying the information on yarns, equipment, pattern instructions, and basic techniques. If you want your knits to be fashionable and flattering, consult the section on choosing colors and styles.

Old hands look here: More experienced knitters can progress to adapting patterns in various ways, and then to designing their own unique knits. Garment shaping, construction, and assembly are explained in detail with clear diagrams and photographs. Textured stitch techniques and the various methods for knitting with several colors are described and shown in detailed photographs, together with the fascinating methods used for circular knitting, patchwork, and entrelac.

There's a section on more experimental techniques, too: try felting, dyeing, and embellishing your knits with embroidery, beads, crochet, and knitted trims.

On most pages you'll find tips, ideas to try, and helpful hints on sorting out problems. With a comprehensive index, you can easily find the topic you want—or just browse the pages to find an exciting new technique for your next experiment.

Happy knitting

Betty Barnden

About this book

Try it panels:
these regular companion features contain great ideas for experimenting with methods and materials, plus exciting projects for practicing and developing new skills and techniques

Step-by-step sequences:
presented in the number of stages needed to work a given knitting technique, these help you learn new skills and brush up on old ones

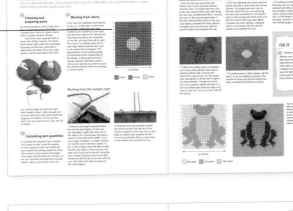

Design ideas:
dozens of suggestions for embellishments, from necklines and edgings to knit-in motifs

Fix it panels:
these regular companion features contain handy hints for repairing your work and avoiding common knitting pitfalls

Completed swatches:
fully worked swatches show you what the finished stitch pattern will look like

Stitch patterns:
new and classic favorites are fully shown and explained

Fold-out flap:
this feature can be folded out and used to clarify any abbreviations used in the stitch patterns.

EQUIPMENT AND MATERIALS

There's a wealth of needles and accessories for today's knitter to choose from, and a whole world of knitting yarns! The information in this chapter will help you select the equipment you need, and choose suitable yarn for any project you have in mind.

Knitting needles

Knitting needles are obtainable in plastic, metal, bamboo, or wood. The type you choose may be influenced by the yarn you are knitting with and the size of the needle, but you will also be swayed by personal preference.

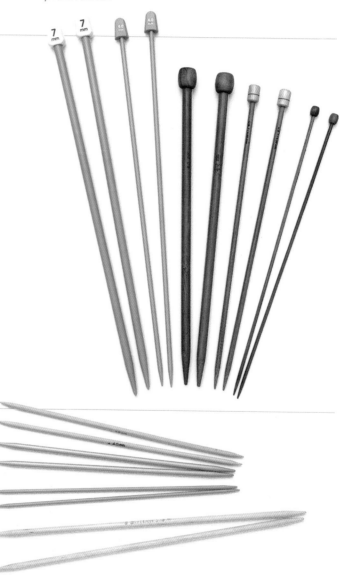

1 Pairs of needles

Needles come in a range of different sizes (diameters) to suit different weights of yarn. They are also available in different lengths from 8in (20cm) to 16in (40cm) to suit the number of stitches required for a particular project. Some knitters always use long needles because they like to knit with the end of one needle tucked under their arm. Others prefer to use the shortest length that will hold the required stitches because the weight of the knitting is then held closer to the hands, making the needles easier to control.
Plastic needles are light in weight, but may quickly become sticky in humid conditions, or when knitting with synthetic yarns.
Metal needles may be either steel or aluminum. These strong materials are particularly suitable for small needle sizes. The very hard, smooth surface of metal needles can be useful when knitting with tough, elastic yarns but some people find the clicking of metal needles irritating.
Wood or bamboo needles are lightweight and some knitters find them less tiring to the hands than either plastic or metal. They are also useful for knitting with slippery yarns because of the slight friction they produce.

2 Double-pointed needles

These are sold in sets of four or five in the same range of sizes and materials as pairs of needles, and in various lengths from 4in (10cm) to about 16in (40cm). They are pointed at both ends and are generally used for circular knitting, when they are particularly suitable for smaller items such as socks and gloves.

3 Circular needles

These have two rigid tips of metal, plastic, wood, or bamboo, joined by a length of plastic cord. The usual sizes are available in a range of lengths from 12in (30cm) to 100in (250cm) or more. See page 102 for how to choose the correct length for your project.

FIX IT

6 *Got a chip in your needle?*

In an emergency you can gently smooth away a small nick on a needle using a fine nail file. However it's best to replace damaged needles as soon as possible.

4 Interchangeable needle kit

Interchangeable kits are available, with several pairs of rigid plastic needle tips and flexible cords of different lengths plus extender pieces (to join two lengths of cord) and end-stops (for putting work aside or using the tips and cords for flat knitting). Such kits are quite expensive, but one kit can provide all the needles you will ever need. However, some people find that the stitches catch on the joins between the tips and cords. If your stitch gauge is quite tight, a set like this may not be ideal for you.

7 Equivalent needle sizes

Choosing the correct size (diameter) of needles is crucial to obtaining correct gauge (see page 20). Needles are sized in the US from 0 to about 20, and in Europe from 2mm to 15mm or more. There is not an exact match between the two systems. You can use needles sized by either system, provided you check your gauge carefully.

US	Europe
0	2mm
1	2.25mm
3	3mm
4	3.25mm
5	3.5mm
6	4mm
7	4.5mm
8	5mm
9	5.5mm
10	6mm
10.5	6.5 or 7mm
11	8mm
13	9mm
15	10mm
17	12 or 13mm
20	15mm

5 Arthritic hands

If you have arthritis or other problems with your hands, look out for casein needles. These look like ivory or tortoiseshell, are non-conductible, lightweight, warm, quiet, and smooth, enabling fast knitting. Casein is actually made from skimmed milk so it is a natural and biodegradable material.

8 Needle care

Keep needles clean and dry, and stored flat with the points protected. Never store them standing on their points in a pot or jar. Keep plastic needles away from heat and direct sunlight. If a needle becomes sticky it can be washed in warm water if it is made of plastic or aluminum; if it is made of wood or bamboo, wipe it with a damp cloth and dry with a towel.

Additional equipment

There are a few basic items that you need to complete any knitting project: tape measure, scissors, pins, and a tapestry needle. In addition there are times when you require other items, such as a stitch holder, ring marker, or row counter; these items can be purchased as they are required. Here is a brief description of what you might need.

Pins

Large-headed pins are the best type to use when measuring your gauge (page 20) or assembling a project (page 140) because the large colored heads won't get lost between the stitches.

Tape measure and ruler

A tape measure is used to take body measurements (page 25) and to measure the length of work in progress (page 21); for measuring your gauge (page 20) use a short ruler, which is more precise.

Scissors

Small, sharp scissors are used to cut yarn. Never try to break yarn with your fingers—some yarns are very strong and will cut your skin.

Needle gauge

Most needles now have the size printed on them, but a needle gauge is useful for checking the size of unidentified needles (such as some double-pointed needles).

Tapestry needles

For sewing seams (page 140), running in yarn tails (page 143), and embroidery (page 126–128) you need a blunt-tipped needle with a large eye (like a tapestry needle). These are available in a range of sizes to suit different yarn types. They are sometimes called knitters' needles.

Point protectors

Pairs of plastic point protectors are used when storing needles to avoid damage to the points. They can also be used to prevent stitches from slipping off the needles when you put your work aside.

Get a bag

Knitting needles and accessories can easily go astray, so it is a good idea to keep them in a case, bag, or basket. Choose a design with several small pockets to suit your scissors, tape measure, and other accessories so these may be kept apart from balls of yarn. A knitting basket should always be lined with fabric to avoid snagging the yarns.

Teasel brush

A teasel brush is used to brush up the surface of fluffy yarns such as mohair.

Bobbins

Plastic bobbins are useful when working with several small balls of yarn, for example when working intarsia designs (page 124).

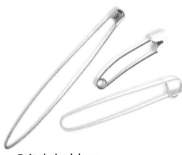

Cable needles

Cable needles are short, double-ended needles used when working cables (page 90). They may be straight, cranked, or hooked; try out the different types to see which you like best.

Crochet hooks

These are available in a range of sizes and in basically the same materials as knitting needles. Use them for working crochet edgings (page 138), for crochet seams (page 144), or for picking up dropped stitches (page 51).

Darning needles

Occasionally a sharp darning needle with a large eye is useful, for example when embroidering on felted knitting (page 116). Again, several sizes are available.

Stitch holders

These devices work like large safety pins, and are used for holding groups of stitches when working necklines (page 72), for example. In fact, you can use a large safety pin for small groups of stitches.

Ring markers

Small plastic rings in various sizes are used to mark a particular place along a row (or round), and are slipped from row to row. Choose a size that fits loosely over the needles so it is easy to slip from one needle tip to the other. Decorative markers are also available. If you don't have a ring marker, simply tie a loop of contrasting yarn to use as a marker.

Split markers

Split-ring markers are slipped onto a completed stitch to mark it, and can be removed and replaced at any time.

Graph paper and drawing equipment

If you want to design your own garments or stitch patterns, you'll need graph paper, pencils, and colored crayons. Ordinary graph paper with 8 or 10 squares to 1in (2.5cm) is a useful size, or you can obtain special knitters' graph paper, with a rectangular grid that corresponds with a typical gauge of stockinette knitting.

Row counters

A row counter can be very useful, especially when working patterns or shapes where several rows need to be repeated over and over. The barrel type is fitted onto a straight needle and pushed along to the knob. For large-sized straight needles, or for circular knitting, you need the clutch type.

Pompom maker

Pompom makers are available in several sizes (page 133).

Antique needles

Before the introduction of European sizing in millimeters (mm), UK and Canadian sizes were formerly numbered from 14 (small) to 000 (large)—the opposite way to US sizes—so a printed size on a thrift-store bargain may be misleading.

Which yarn?

There are so many yarns available today that it's hard to know where to start. Various weights of yarn may be made from a surprisingly large selection of fibers and processed in many ways to produce a wide range of effects.

Yarn weights

Yarn comes in many different thicknesses, called weights, from fine fingering through to extra bulky. The weights are approximations only, varying slightly from one manufacturer to another, but here's a rough guide to help you find the yarn you want.

Extra bulky
Needle size: 11–15 (8–10mm) or larger.
Use for: casual, chunky garments and household articles.
Stitches: simple stitch patterns to avoid excess bulk and weight.
Speed to knit: very quick.

Bulky
Needle size: 10–11 (6–8mm).
Use for: casual garments, household articles.
Stitches: plain or textured (color knits can be too bulky).
Speed to knit: quick.

Worsted/Aran
Needle size: 7–9 (4.5–5.5mm).
Use for: casual, medium-weight garments, household articles.
Stitches: any.
Speed to knit: fairly quick.

Sport/double knitting
Needle size: 4–6 (3.5–4mm).
Use for: casual or tailored medium-weight garments, including babywear.
Stitches: any.
Speed to knit: medium; light to handle.

Fingering/4-ply/3-ply
Needle size: 1–3 (2.25–3.25mm).
Use for: casual or tailored lightweight garments, including babywear.
Stitches: any; good for lace stitches and color knitting.
Speed to knit: quite slow, very light to handle.

Fibers
Many different fibers are used to make yarns, often blended together to improve handle, washability, wear, or price.

Animal: Wool, cashmere, mohair, alpaca, and other animal fibers are spun into yarns that are generally warm, soft, and light. Shrink-resistant types are easier to wash. Silk (spun from the cocoons of silkworms) is smooth, glossy, cool to the touch, and very strong.

Vegetable: Cotton, linen, ramie, hemp, soy, and other fibers derived from plants generally make strong, smooth yarns that may be matte or glossy. Viscose rayon is manufactured from wood cellulose, so it is man-made, but in a sense also a vegetable fiber; it is very smooth and shiny.

Synthetic: Fibers such as acrylics are manufactured from by-products of the petroleum and chemical industries. The new generation of micro-fibers are now often blended with natural fibers to make high-quality yarns that are economical and easy to wash.

12

Fancy yarns

Different fibers may be spun and processed in a variety of ways to make yarn. These yarn types have a wide range of weights and constituents, so here's a selection to whet your appetite:

Ribbon/Tape
A flat, woven tape (this example is cotton/viscose and shade-dyed).
Stitches: plain stitches—others tend to lose their effect.

Mohair
Light, fluffy yarn—brush gently to raise pile.
Stitches: bold textures or lace patterns (subtle stitch patterns will not show up).

Bouclé
Spun with little loops and curls (this example is spot-dyed).
Stitches: simple stitch patterns, bold textures e.g. cables.

Tweed
Contains little flecks of contrasting colors.
Stitches: any; suits subtle color patterns.

Chenille
Soft, velvety texture.
Stitches: plain stitches, bold textures, color work.

Silk
Smooth, luxurious yarn with a soft sheen (this example is hand-dyed).
Stitches: any, but avoid loose stitch patterns, which may "drop."

Slub
Thick-and-thin spun yarn (this example in cotton).
Stitches: plain stitches, bold textures.

Metallic
Sometimes called lurex.
Stitches: plain stitches, bold textures, color work.

⊚TRY IT

13 Alternative materials

You can knit with long lengths of any flexible material: try string, fine wire, raffia, or anything else you can find.

Tear lightweight cotton fabrics into strips about ¾in (2cm) wide. Join the strips with simple knots, or overlap the ends and sew them together. Use needles size 11 (8mm) or larger.

Cut lightweight plastic bags into strips of fairly equal width (a spiral cut makes a continuous strip).

These bracelets are knitted with metallic elastic (from a florist's shop), and with fishing line threaded with beads (see page 130).

Buying yarn

Some knitters start with a design and then find the right yarn to make it; others buy yarns on impulse and then decide what to make. Whichever type of knitter you are, here's the information you need to choose wisely.

14

Reading ball bands

Most yarns now have bands that give you the information you need to make the right choice for any project—details about fiber content, recommended needle size, length of yarn on each ball, and washing instructions, for example.

Gauge/tension guide gives the recommended gauge for the yarn (see page 20).

Yardage and weight. Some fibers are heavier than others so, for example, 2 oz (50gm) of cotton yarn may well be shorter in length than 2 oz (50gm) of woolen yarn with a similar recommended gauge.

Care instructions are usually provided as symbols that tell you if the yarn can be hand- or machine-washed, dry-cleaned, pressed, and so on (see page 150). Keep a ball band from each project for future reference, and if the item is a gift, make sure you pass on the details.

Recommended needle size for stockinette stitch.

Fiber content (see page 14).

If purchasing more than one ball of the same color, make sure the dye-lot numbers match because any slight difference may become visible once the yarn is knitted up.

⊚TRY IT

16 **Keep notes**

Keep a scrapbook of ball bands from all your projects, together with your notes and photographs, as an invaluable reference for future knitting projects, washing garments, etc.

17 **Pass it on**

If you knit someone a gift, make an accompanying label (or greeting card) carrying the care instructions from the ball band.

15

Yarn buyer's checklist

If you are working from a pattern book or leaflet:

• Consult the instructions and buy the correct amount for the required size of the exact yarn specified, making sure that all the dye-lot numbers match for each color needed.
• If you want to make any pattern alteration involving extra knitting (such as longer sleeves), buy an extra ball or two.

To substitute a different yarn in a pattern book or leaflet:

• Find a substitute yarn that matches the original as closely as possible in yardage, fiber content, and gauge, or see below.
• If the yardage does not match, calculate the total yardage of original yarn required. The quoted number of balls x original yardage = total yardage. Divide this number by the substitute yardage to find the number of substitute balls you need.
• If the fiber content does not match, consider whether the substitute yarn will drape in the same way as the original, and how it will feel in wear: for example, a summer top designed to be knitted in a silk or cotton yarn may be perfectly feasible in a substitute woolen yarn, but the result would be warmer to wear and springier, without the drape of a non-elastic yarn.
• If the gauge does not match, you will need to make adjustments to the instructions to compensate. For a difference in row gauge (measured lengthwise), simply work more or fewer

rows to match the measurements required for different parts of the design. However, if the stitch gauge (measured widthwise) does not match, this can be tricky and another substitute should be considered. In either case, it is wise to buy an extra ball or two.
• Buy an extra ball anyway—you can always make a hat.

When designing or adapting patterns:

• If possible, consult existing pattern books/leaflets for the chosen yarn, to find a pattern similar to what you intend to design and make. Buy the specified amount of yarn, plus 10–15% extra.
• Another way is to buy just one ball and make a whole ball test piece: Using the needle size(s) you intend to use, cast on 50 stitches and work in the pattern you intend to use until the whole ball is used up. Make the sample representative of your project: if half the project will be in a textured stitch, or on smaller needles, make the sample the same way. Measure the test piece, for example, 10 x 12in = 120in square (25 x 30cm = 750cm square).

Now calculate the area of the knitted pieces for your project: Suppose you are making a sweater of the measurements shown below.

The total area of the back, front and two sleeves = 440 + 440 + 234 + 234in = 1348in square (2750 + 2750 + 1462 + 1462 = 8424cm square). Add 15% extra to allow for inaccuracies in estimation and for details such as neckbands: 1348 x 115% = 1550in square (8424 x 115% = 9687cm square).

To find the number of balls required, divide this final total by the area of the test piece. For example, 1550 divided by 120 = 12.9 (9687 divided by 750 = 12.9). So for our example, you would need to buy 13 balls of yarn. You may finish the project with yarn left over, but all knitters need a stash.

Buying online:

The Internet has transformed the availability of knitting yarns: you can now buy all the yarns you will ever need from sources all over the world, without leaving home. Some sites provide online ordering, others an online catalogue for a mail-order service. Always observe the following precautions:
• Only buy online from secure sites.
• Colors on screen can be deceptive—it may be possible to order a color swatch card, which causes some delay but saves expensive mistakes.
• You can't feel the texture of a yarn on screen. Again, ordering a swatch card, or a sample ball, can save time and money in the end.
• If you want more detail about a yarn, such as the recommended gauge, or the yardage, e-mail the company with your query before purchasing.

Conversions
• Centimeters x 0.394 = inches
• Grams x 0.035 = ounces
• Inches x 2.54 = centimeters
• Ounces x 28.6 = grams
• Meters x 1.1 = yards
• Yards x 0.91 = meters

Equivalent weights
• $^{3}/_{4}$ oz = 20 g
• 1 oz = 28 g
• $1^{1}/_{2}$ oz = 40 g
• $1^{3}/_{4}$ oz = 50 g
• 2 oz = 60 g
• $3^{1}/_{2}$ oz = 100 g

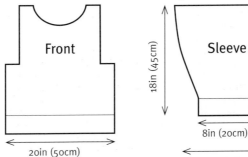

Approximate area:
20 x 22in = 440in square
(50 x 55cm = 2750cm square)

Back

22in (55cm)

20in (50cm)

Approximate area: as back

Front

22in (55cm)

20in (50cm)

18in (45cm)

Sleeve

18in (45cm)

8in (20cm)

average 13in (32.5cm)

Approximate area:
18 x 13in = 234in square
(45 x 32.5cm = 1462cm square)

PATTERNS AND CHARTS

Knitting instructions can seem daunting at first. However, once you're familiar with the conventions of abbreviations and charts, and you understand the importance of correct gauge (and how to obtain it), you'll be able to follow any pattern with confidence.

Following a knitting pattern

The following information should help you understand the pattern better.

Multiple sizes (1)

If a pattern comes in different sizes, these will be set out in order from the smallest to the largest, either in a grid or with the larger sizes in brackets (see garment pieces, right). Some patterns include measurements in both inches and centimeters: these two systems do not correspond exactly, so choose which system you want to follow and use it for the whole project.

Yarn and other materials (2)

It is best to buy the exact yarn specified. If you want to substitute a different yarn, see page 16. Always buy all the yarn required for your chosen size at the same time to avoid problems caused by different dye lots.

Abbreviations (3)

Most knitting patterns include a list of abbreviations. These will differ from one source to another: "K1b," for example, may mean "knit one in the back of the stitch" (through the back loop), or it may mean "knit one in color b," or even "knit one in the row below." Always read the abbreviations carefully and familiarize yourself with them. A list of common abbreviations is given on page 154.

Gauge (4)

It is most important to check your gauge, as described on page 20, and match it exactly to the gauge given in the instructions.

Woolly Lattice & Cable Trapeze Sweater

Please read all the instructions and the pattern carefully before starting to knit the design.
Use the close up and front cover images as an additional guide.

	1	Small	Medium	Large
To fit bust	cm	91	102	107
	in	36	40	42
Actual bust measurement	cm	103	113	120
	in	40½	44½	47½
Length from shoulder approximately	cm	56	58	61
	in	22	23	24
Sleeve Length	cm	40	40	40
	in	15¾	15¾	15¾
2 Yarn - DMC Woolly 50gm balls shade 112		18	20	22

3 Abbreviations

beg - beginning
cm - centimeter
cont - continue
foll - following
g - grams
in - inch
inc - increase
k - knit
k2tog - knit 2 sts together
k3tog - knit 3 sts together
mm - millimeter
p - purl
p2tog - purl 2 sts together
patt - pattern
rem - remaining
rep - repeat
RS - right side
sl 1-k1-psso - slip 1 st, knit 1 st, pass slipped st over the knit st
sl 1-k2tog-psso - slip 1 st, knit 2 sts together, pass slipped stitch over
sm - slip marker
st(s) - stitch(es)
st st - stockinette stitch
WS - wrong side
yo - yarn over needle
( ) - work instructions within brackets as many times as directed
[ ] - different sizes and total stitches
***** - repeat the instructions following the single asterisk as directed

Special Abbreviations
C8F - slip next 4 sts on to a cable needle at front of work, k4, then k4 from cable needle
C8B - slip next 4 sts on to a cable needle at back of work, k, then k4 from cable needle

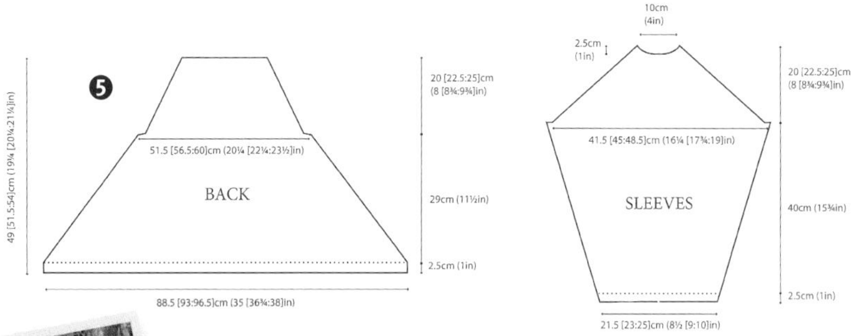
5
49 [51.5:54]cm (19¼ [20¼:21¼]in)
51.5 [56.5:60]cm (20¼ [22¼:23½]in)
BACK
20 [22.5:25]cm (8 [8¾:9¾]in)
29cm (11½in)
2.5cm (1in)
88.5 [93:96.5]cm (35 [36¾:38]in)
10cm (4in)
2.5cm (1in)
20 [22.5:25]cm (8 [8¾:9¾]in)
41.5 [45:48.5]cm (16¼ [17¾:19]in)
SLEEVES
40cm (15¾in)
2.5cm (1in)
21.5 [23:25]cm (8½ [9:10]in)

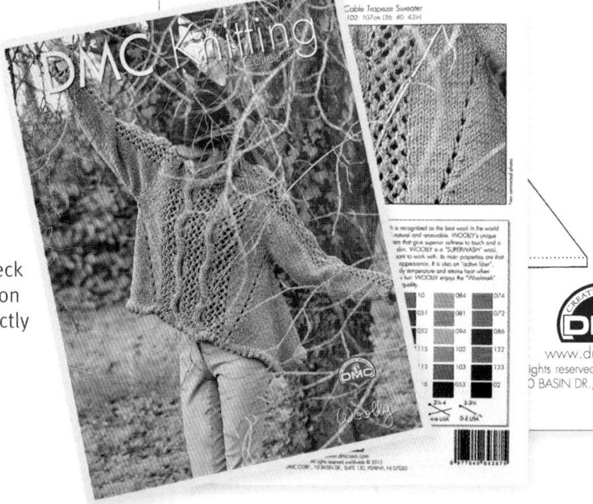
DMC Knitting
Woolly

Level: Advanced

Needles
A pair of US11 (8mm/UK0) knitting needles
Stitch markers
Yarn needle to darn in ends

Gauge 4
12 sts and 16 rows =4"x4" measured over stockinette stitch using US11 (8mm/UK0) needles and 3 strands of yarn held together.
Check your gauge - if less stitches or rows use smaller needles, if more use larger needles.
IT IS ESSENTIAL TO WORK TO THE STATED GAUGE TO ENSURE SUCCESS.
Cable panel (worked over 36 sts)

www.dmc-usa.com
ights reserved worldwide © 2015
O BASIN DR., SUITE 130, KEARNY, NJ 07032

Garment pieces (5)

As a rule, it is best to work the pieces in the order given because there may be a reason why they are in that order. For example, a pocket lining may need to be worked before knitting a front.

Measurement diagrams Some knitting patterns include measurement diagrams, which can be very helpful. Always check the measurement of each piece you knit against any measurements given.

Where different figures apply to different sizes, the figures for the larger sizes are usually given in brackets. For example, "cast on 48 [56, 64] stitches," means cast on 48 stitches for the small size, 56 stitches for the medium size and 64 stitches for the large size. Where only one figure is given, this applies to all sizes. For example: "Bind off 6 stitches at beginning of next row" applies to whatever size you are making.

Repeats (6)

Two kinds of repeat are commonly used in knitting patterns:

Stitch repeats: These may be indicated by brackets, for example "(K2, P1) 3 times" means K2, P1, K2, P1, K2, P1.

Stitch repeats may also be indicated by asterisks, for example " * K2, P1, * repeat from * to * to last stitch, K1" means K2, P1, then repeat these 3 stitches over and over until you reach the last stitch of the row, K1.

Stitch repeats are also sometimes given in chart form, see page 22.

Section repeats: Sometimes a whole section of instructions may be repeated—for example the instructions for a sweater front might read "work as given for Back to ** ," meaning "Follow the instructions for the back until you reach the symbol ** ," at which point, you should return to the instructions for the Front to continue working. Sometimes sections are repeated several times.

Shaping (7)

Some instructions tell you in detail exactly how to work increasing and/ or decreasing, whereas others may be more vague. For example, "K2tog at beginning of every right side row" tells you what decreasing method to use, whereas "decrease 1 stitch at beginning of every right side row" leaves the knitter to decide what method to use; in this case, consult page 54–59 to choose a suitable method.

Assembly and blocking (8)

This is sometimes called "Making up" or "Finishing." Assemble the pieces in the order given. Instructions rarely give details of the type of seam(s) to use, so consult pages 140–147. Follow the instructions given if you have used the exact yarn specified. Otherwise, consult the yarn ball band and block or press accordingly (see page 148).

---

❻

Row 1: K1, * (yo, sl 1-k1-psso) 3 times, k8 *; rep from * to * once more, (yo, sl 1-k1-psso) 3 times, k1.

Row 2 and every foll WS row: P to end.

Row 3: K1, * (sl 1-k1-psso, yo) 3 times, k8 *; rep from * to * once more, (sl 1-k1-psso, yo) 3 times, k1.

Row 5: K1, * (yo, sl 1-k1-psso) 3 times, C8F *; rep from * to * once more, (yo, sl 1-k1-psso) 3 times, k1.

Row 7: As row 3.
Row 9: As row 1.
Row 11: As row 3.
Row 13: As row 1.

Row 15: K1, * (sl 1-k1-psso, yo) 3 times, C8B * ; rep from * to * once more, (sl 1-k1-psso, yo) 3 times, k1.

Row 17: As row 1.
Row 19: As row 3.
Row 20: P to end.
These 20 rows form the cable panel and are repeated.

NOTE: the sweater is worked using 3 strands of yarn held together to make a thicker yarn. Always ensure that the needle is inserted through all 3 strands for each stitch.

BACK
Using US11 needles and 3 strands of yarn held together, cast on 106 [112:116] sts.
Work 4 rows in st st (1 row k, 1 row p) starting with a k row.
Next Row (hem fold line): K1, * k2tog, yo; rep from * to last st, k1.
Next Row: P to end.

Commence cable panel and eyelet shaping
Row 1: K21 [24:26], place a stitch marker on needle, k11, yo, sl 1-k1-psso, k1, place a stitch marker on needle, work row 1 of cable panel, place a stitch marker on needle, k1, k2tog, yo, k11, place a stitch marker on needle, k21 [24:26]. Markers divide patt panels.

Row 2 and every foll WS row: P to end, slipping markers.

Row 3: Sl 1-k1-psso, k19 [22:24], slip marker, k14, slip marker, work row 3 of cable panel, slip marker, k14, slip marker, k19 [22:24], k2tog. 104 [110:114] sts

Row 5: Sl 1-k1-psso, k18 [21:23], sm, k10, yo, sl 1-k1-psso, k2, sm, work row 5 of cable panel, sm, k2, k2tog, yo, k10, sm, k18 [21:23], k2tog. 102 [108:112] sts

Row 7: Sl 1-k1-psso, k17 [20:22], sm, k14, sm, work row 7 of cable panel, sm, k14, sm, k17 [20:22], k2tog. 100 [106:110] sts

Row 9: Sl 1-k1-psso, k16 [19:21], sm, k9, yo, sl 1-k1-psso, k3, sm, work row 9 of cable panel, sm, k3, k2tog, yo, k9, sm, k16 [19:21], k2tog. 98 [104:108] sts

Row 11: Sl 1-k1-psso, k15 [18:20], sm, k14, sm, work row 11 of cable panel, sm, k14, sm, k15 [18:20], k2tog. 96 [102:106] sts

Row 13: Sl 1-k1-psso, k14 [17:19], sm, k8, yo, sl 1-k1-psso, k4, sm, work row 13 of cable panel, sm, k4, k2tog, yo, k8, sm, k14 [17:19], k2tog. 94 [100:104] sts

Row 15: Sl 1-k1-psso, k13 [16:18], sm, k14, sm, work row 15 of cable panel, sm, k14, sm, k13 [16:18], k2tog. 92 [98:102] sts

Row 17: Sl 1-k1-psso, k12 [15:17], sm, k7, yo, sl 1-k1-psso, k5, sm, work row 17 of cable panel, sm, k5, k2tog, yo, k7, sm, k12 [15:17], k2tog. 90 [96:100] sts

Row 19: Sl 1-k1-psso, k11 [14:16], sm, k14, sm, work row 19 of cable panel, sm, k11 [14:16], k2tog. 88 [94:98] sts

Row 21: Sl 1-k1-psso, k10 [13:15], sm, k6, yo, sl 1-k1-psso, k6, sm, work row 1 of cable panel, sm, k6, k2tog, yo, k6, sm, k10 [13:15], k2tog. 86 [92:96] sts

Row 23: Sl 1-k1-psso, k9 [12:14], sm, k14, sm, work row 3 of cable panel, sm, k14, sm, k9

[12:14], k2tog. 84 [90:94] sts

Row 25: Sl 1-k1-psso, k8 [11:13], sm, k5, yo, sl 1-k1-psso, k7, sm, work row 5 of cable panel, sm, k7, k2tog, yo, k5, sm, k8 [11:13], k2tog. 82 [88:92] sts

Row 27: Sl 1-k1-psso, k7 [10:12], sm, k14, sm, work row 7 of cable panel, sm, k14, sm, k7 [10:12], k2tog. 80 [86:90] sts

Row 29: Sl 1-k1-psso, k6 [9:11], sm, k4, yo, sl 1-k1-psso, k8, sm, work row 9 of cable panel, sm, k8, k2tog, yo, k4, sm, k6 [9:11], k2tog. 78 [84:88] sts

Row 31: Sl 1-k1-psso, k5 [8:10], sm, k14, sm, work row 11 of cable panel, sm, k14, sm, k5 [8:10], k2tog. 76 [82:86] sts

Row 33: Sl 1-k1-psso, k4 [7:9], sm, k3, yo, sl 1-k1-psso, k9, sm, work row 13 of cable panel, sm, k9, k2tog, yo, k3, sm, k4 [7:9], k2tog. 74 [80:84] sts

Row 35: Sl 1-k1-psso, k3 [6:8], sm, k14, sm, work row 15 of cable panel, sm, k14, sm, k3 [6:8], k2tog. 72 [78:82] sts

Row 37: Sl 1-k1-psso, k2 [5:7], sm, k2, yo, sl 1-k1-psso, k10, sm, work row 17 of cable panel, sm, k10, k2tog, yo, k2, sm, k2 [5:7], k2tog. 70 [76:80] sts

Row 39: Sl 1-k1-psso, k1 [4:6], sm, k14, sm, work row 19 of cable panel, sm, k14, sm, k1 [4:6], k2tog. 68 [74:78] sts

Row 41: Sl 1-k1-psso, k0 [3:5], remove marker, k1, yo, sl 1-k1-psso, k11, sm, work row 1 of cable panel, sm, k11, k2tog, yo, k1, remove marker, k0 [3:5], k2tog. 66 [72:76] sts

Row 43: Sl 1-k1-psso, k13 [16:18], sm, work row 3 of cable panel, sm, k13 [16:18], k2tog. 64 [70:74] sts

Row 45: Sl 1-k1-psso, k12 [15:17], sm, work row 5 of cable panel, sm, k12 [15:17], k2tog. 62 [68:72] sts

Row 46: P to end, slipping markers.

Shape raglan armholes
Next Row: Bind off 2 [3:3] sts, k to marker, sm, work row 7 of cable panel, sm, k to end.
Next Row: Bind off 2 [3:3] sts, p to end, slipping markers. 58 [62:66] sts **

Row 1: K3, k3tog, k to marker, sm, work row 9 cable panel, sm, k to last 6 sts, sl 1-k2tog-psso, k3.

Row 2: P to end, slipping markers.

Row 3: K to marker, sm, work row 11 of cable panel, sm, k to end.

Row 4: P to end, slipping markers.

Keeping cable and eyelet panels correct as far as possible and always working 3 sts in st st at each end, rep rows 1 to 4 until 26 sts remain, ending with row 2.

Bind off. **❻**

FRONT
Work as given for Back to **. 58 [62:66] sts

Row 1: K3, k3tog, k to marker, sm, work row 9 of cable panel, sm, k to last 6 sts, sl 1-k2tog-psso, k3.

Row 2: P to end, slipping markers.

Row 3: K to marker, sm, work row 11 of cable panel, sm, k to end.

Row 4: P to end, slipping markers.

Keeping cable and eyelet panels correct as far as possible and always working 3 sts in st st at each end, rep rows 1 to 4 until 34 sts remain, ending with row 2.

Shape front neck
Next Row: K3, patt 9 sts, bind off 10 sts, patt to last 3 sts, k3.
Work each side of the neck separately.
Next Row (WS): P to end. 12 sts
Next Row: Bind off 2 sts at beg (neck edge), patt to last 6 sts, sl 1-k2tog-psso, k3. 8 sts
Next Row: P to end.
Next Row: Bind off 2 sts, patt to last 3 sts, k3. 6 sts
Next Row: Patt to last 2 sts, p2tog. 5 sts
P 1 row.
Next Row: Sl 1-k2tog, psso, k2. 3 sts
P 1 row.
Bind off.

With WS of work facing, rejoin yarn to rem 12 sts.
Next Row (WS): Bind off 2 sts at beg (neck edge), p to end. 10 sts
Next Row: K3, k3tog, k to end. 8 sts
Next Row: Bind off 2 sts, p to end. 6 sts
Next Row: K3, patt to end.
Next Row: P2tog, p to end. 5 sts
Next Row: K2, k3tog. 3 sts
P 1 row.
Bind off.

SLEEVES (both alike)
NOTE: the cable panel is worked over the center 22 sts. Work the 20 row cable panel but repeat from * to * once only.
Using US11 needles and 3 strands of yarn held together, cast on 26 [28:30] sts.
Work 4 rows in st st, starting with a k row.
Next Row (hem fold line): K1, * k2tog, yo; rep from * to last st, k1.
Next Row: P to end.

Commence cable panel and shaping
Row 1: K2 [3:4], place a stitch marker on needle, work row 1 of cable panel working from * to * once only, place a stitch marker on needle, k2 [3:4]. Markers divide cable panel and st st.
Row 2 and every foll WS row: P to end, slipping markers.
Cont to work cable panel as set AT THE SAME TIME inc 1 st at each end of next and every foll 4th row (bringing inc sts into st st) to 50 [54:58] sts.
Cont in patt without shaping until sleeve measures 42cm (17in), ending with a WS row.

Shape raglan
Keeping cable panel correct, bind off 2 sts at beg of next 2 rows. 46 [50:54] sts
Row 1: K3, k3tog, k to marker, sm, work cable panel, sm, k to last 6 sts, sl 1-k2tog-psso, k3.
Row 2: P to end, slipping markers.
Row 3: K to marker, sm, work cable panel, sm, k to end.
Row 4: P to end, slipping markers.
Keeping cable panel and eyelet panels correct as far as possible and always working 3 sts in st st at each end, rep rows 1 to 4 until 18 sts remain, ending with row 2.

Shape top
Next Row: Patt 5 sts, bind off 8 sts, patt to end.
Work each side separately.
Next Row (WS): P to last 2 sts, p2tog. 4 sts
Next Row: K3tog, k1. 2 sts
P 1 row.
Bind off.
With WS of work facing, rejoin yarn to rem 5 sts.
Next Row (WS): P2tog, p to end. 4 sts
Next Row: Sl 1-k2tog-psso, k1. 2 sts
P 1 row.
Bind off.

FINISHING
Sew in all yarn ends neatly. Block or press the pieces according to instructions on ball band. Join front raglan seams. Join right back raglan seam.

Collar
With RS of work facing, using US11 needles and 3 strands of yarn held together, pick up and k 14 sts around top of left sleeve, 7 sts down side of front neck, 10 sts across front neck, 7 sts up side of front neck, 14 sts around top of right sleeve and 26 sts across back neck. 78 sts
Next Row (WS): P2, * k2, p2; rep from * to end.
Next Row: K2, * p2, k2; rep from * to end.
Rep these 2 rows until collar measures 20cm (8in). Bind off in rib.
Join back raglan seam. Join collar, reversing seam for turn back. Join side and sleeve seams. Fold hems on lower edge to the WS along eyelet row and slip stitch in place.

❼

❽

Measuring your gauge

Correct gauge is the key to successful knitting. Gauge (sometimes called "tension") is a measure of the number of stitches and rows to a given measurement, often 4in (10cm). Your knitted garment won't fit if it isn't knitted to the correct gauge, so the importance of getting the gauge right cannot be over-emphasized.

A knitting pattern designer uses the gauge to calculate how many stitches and rows are needed to make a knitted piece of the required size. If you knit to the gauge stated in the pattern, your knitted item should turn out as expected.

A typical gauge for a bulky yarn might be "16 stitches and 20 rows to 4in (10cm) using size US 10 (6mm) needles and stockinette stitch." Such a gauge is often quoted on a ball band, sometimes in the form of a diagram, this gauge being chosen by the manufacturer as giving the best performance in terms of stability and drape. However the designer may recommend smaller or larger needles than the size suggested on the ball band, perhaps to produce a denser or looser stitch for a particular look or purpose.

Factors affecting gauge

Never assume that your own gauge will be correct. There are a number of interacting variables that may affect your gauge:
The thickness of the yarn: It's easy to understand that a fine 4-ply yarn will knit up with smaller stitches than a heavy, bulky yarn.
The yarn fiber: Some fibers are less flexible than others, so two yarns of the same weight (e.g. Aran or worsted weight) may knit to different gauges—a softer yarn will often knit more tightly than a firm yarn.
Needle size and type: The larger the needle size, the larger the stitches made. However, the material of the needles may also affect gauge—very smooth metal needles may produce a slightly tighter gauge than wood or bamboo needles of the same size.
Stitch pattern: Gauge is normally quoted over stockinette stitch, but where a knitting pattern uses another stitch pattern as the main stitch, the gauge should be quoted over that stitch. For example, a garter-stitch gauge will have a few less stitches and a lot more rows to 4in (10cm) than a stockinette-stitch gauge obtained with the same yarn and needles.
Your technique: There are several ways to hold yarn and needles. Your own method (and even your mood) can affect your gauge.
For all these reasons, it is important always to check your gauge before beginning any project, as below.

Making a gauge swatch

Consult the instructions to find the recommended gauge. A typical example might read "18 stitches and 22 rows to 4in (10cm) using size US 8 (5mm) needles and stockinette stitch." Make a swatch piece that you expect to measure about 6 x 6in (15 x 15cm). In our example, cast on 27 or 28 stitches and work 33 or 34 rows of stockinette stitch before binding off. Follow the instructions in the pattern (or on the ball band) to press or block the swatch in the same way as the finished article.

1 | Lay the swatch on a flat surface. Using a ruler or tape measure, place two pins exactly 4in (10cm) apart at the center of the swatch, as shown. Count the number of stitches (including any half stitches) along a straight row between the pins.

2 | Now place the pins 4in (10cm) apart vertically and count the number of rows between them, along a straight line of stitches.

• If you have too many rows or stitches, your knitting is too tight. Make another swatch with larger needles.
• If you have too few rows or stitches, your knitting is too loose. Make another swatch with smaller needles.

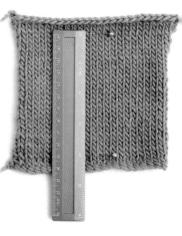

To knit the project, use the same needles that you used to knit the gauge swatch.

3 | Once you have made a swatch that matches the recommended gauge you can start knitting your project, confident that the final result will be the right size. Use the same pair of needles that you used for the swatch. If you need larger (or smaller) needles to match the gauge, you should use correspondingly larger (or smaller) needles for other parts of the pattern where the needle size is changed, for example, for the ribbing.

Measuring work in progress

Measuring the width of your work while it is still on the needles is never accurate, that is why obtaining the correct gauge beforehand is so important. However, pattern instructions often tell you to work to a particular length. Place the knitting on a flat surface and measure the length at the center. Never measure at the side edges.

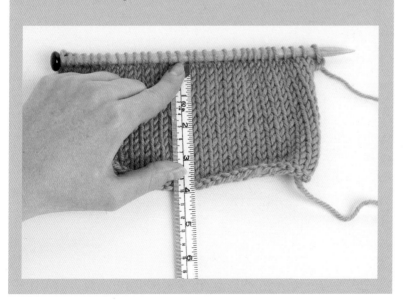

FIX IT

21 *Can't obtain the correct gauge?*

Try leaving your swatches flat overnight—some yarns (especially synthetics) take a few hours to relax or contract into their natural form. Measure the swatches again the next day. Otherwise, it may be possible to add or omit a few rows to adjust to the length of knitting required: try to do this where the knitting is unshaped, e.g. after completing the increasing for a tapered sleeve, but before beginning the shaping for the sleeve top.

Understanding charts and symbols

Sometimes knitting pattern instructions use charts instead of words to explain a stitch pattern. Once you understand the basic principles, this visual method of representation is easy to follow. Two-color knitting, textured knitting, intarsia, and mosaic knitting may all be charted in slightly different ways, as described below.

22

Color knitting charts

Techniques for color knitting are described on pages 122–123. Each small square on the chart represents one stitch. Color-pattern knitting is usually worked in stockinette stitch (all right side rows are knitted, and all wrong side rows are purled). The chart represents the right side of the work.

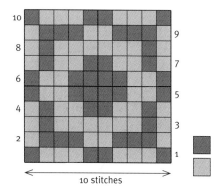

Color A

Color B

← 10 stitches →

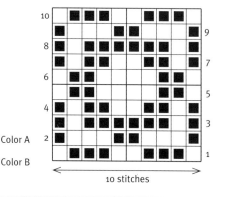

← 10 stitches →

Charts may be printed in color, or symbols may be used to indicate the different colors. Right-side rows (odd numbers) are numbered on the right of the chart, and read from right to left, while wrong-side rows (even numbers) are numbered on the left, and read from left to right. This design has a stitch repeat of 10 stitches, so it requires a multiple of 10 stitches (such as 30, 50, or 120) on the needles.

☐ Color A

 Color B

Stitch repeats

Small charts, like those shown for two-color, textured, and mosaic knitting, are designed to be repeated across the width of the knitting. The number of stitches to be repeated is called the "stitch repeat."

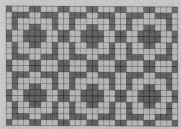

The two-color chart shown above is repeated three times widthwise and twice lengthwise, making 30 stitches x 20 rows.

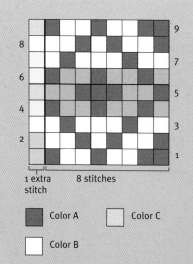

1 extra stitch   8 stitches

■ Color A   ☐ Color C

☐ Color B

Some repeating patterns for two-color knitting, textured knitting, or mosaic knitting require extra stitches at one or both edges to balance the pattern, usually indicated by printing in a paler shade (or using a different symbol). This two-color design requires a multiple of 8 stitches plus 1, such as (3 x 8) + 1 = 25 stitches, or (10 x 8) +1 = 81 stitches.

To repeat this design:
Row 1: Reading chart row 1 from right to left, knit the 8 repeating stitches: K * 2A, 2B, 1A, 2B, 1A *, repeat from * to * to the last stitch, then knit the extra stitch on the left: K1A.
Row 2: Reading chart row 2 from left to right, purl the extra stitch at left: P 1A, then purl the 8 repeating stitches: * 2B, 1A, 1B, 1A, 2B, 1A * repeat from * to * to end.
Continue in this way, reading from successive chart rows.

23

Textured knitting charts

Charts may be used to represent textured stitches such as lace or cable patterns. In fact, almost any stitch formation can be presented in chart form. Each type of stitch (stockinette, bobble, K2tog, yo, etc) is represented by a different symbol. Charts from different sources may use different symbols for the stitch formations, so always consult the chart key. A list of common symbols is given on page 155.

As on a color knitting chart, each square represents one stitch, and the chart represents the right side of the work. Right and wrong side rows are numbered as for a color knitting chart, and read in the same way, right side rows from right to left, and wrong side rows from left to right.

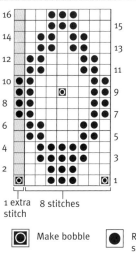

1 extra stitch   8 stitches

Reading a textured knitting chart

Here, a blank square represents stockinette stitch, so on a right-side row a blank square is knitted while on a wrong side row it is purled. A dot represents reverse stockinette stitch, so on a right-side row a dot is purled, but on a wrong side row it is knitted. This design has a stitch repeat of 8 stitches, plus 1, and is worked as follows:

Row 1: * Make bobble, K2, P3, K2, * repeat from * to * to last stitch, make bobble.

Row 2: P1, * P2, K3, P3, * repeat from * to * to end.

Continue in this way reading from successive chart rows.

| ⊙ | Make bobble | ● | Reverse stockinette stitch | □ | Stockinette stitch |

24

Intarsia charts

Intarsia (picture) knitting is described on page 124. Intarsia charts are not designed as repeats but as single motifs or large pictures, normally worked in stockinette stitch. The chart may show the whole width of the knitting (for example, a sweater front), or a rectangular panel, to be placed where required. Each square on the chart represents one stitch, and the chart represents the right side of the work, so right-side rows (odd numbers) are read from right to left, and wrong-side rows (even numbers) from left to right.

18 stitches

Reading an intarsia chart

This chart is designed to be knitted as a panel 18 stitches wide and 26 rows deep, which could be placed anywhere on a sweater front, for example, or perhaps at the center of a pillow. Notice how the chart is drawn on a rectangular grid to match the typical gauge ratio of stockinette stitch. If this bird motif were charted on a square grid, it would appear distorted.

▨	Color A
▨	Color B
●	French knot in black

25

Mosaic knitting charts

Mosaic knitting, using slip stitches, is described in detail on page 121. Charts for mosaic knitting are read in a different way to any of the charts above so the rows are numbered differently.

26

Working circular knitting

Color knitting designs and textured stitches may be adapted for circular knitting as described on page 107.

FIX IT

27 *Confused by a chart?*

Tape a small length of each color to the chart key as an instant reminder. If you keep losing your place when reading a chart, take a photocopy (enlarging the chart if you wish) and mark off each row as you complete it.

Selecting the right size

When you buy an outfit from a store, you buy the size that fits you best and have to accept that if, say, you have fairly long arms, the sleeves are rarely going to reach your wrist. When you knit you have the opportunity to tailor your garment for the most flattering fit, so don't skip the measuring stage.

To determine the size to make from a knitting pattern, compare your body measurements with the size measurements given in the instructions. If the instructions include measurements in both inches and centimeters, choose which system you want to use, and keep to it throughout.

28 Ease

Ease is the difference between a body measurement and the actual size of the finished garment. This extra amount is added for comfort and style. It is normally added to widthwise measurements only, not to lengthwise measurements. The finished size of a jacket or similar garment is measured with any fastenings (such as buttons) closed.
Different amounts of ease may be used in calculating knitting instructions, depending on how closely or loosely the garment is intended to fit. For very close-fitting garments, ease is subtracted from the body measurement, rather than added to it.
Choosing a size to knit When choosing which size to knit, look at the given measurement for the finished size, sometimes called the "actual size." Deduct the given body measurement from the finished size to find the amount of ease included in the pattern. You may decide that the fit is too tight or loose for your liking. For example, if the instructions are for a close-fitting sweater, you may prefer to knit one size larger to make a sweater with a looser fit.

Now check that the length measurements will suit you: measure off the given garment length against the body. Check the sleeve length in the same way. If you need to lengthen or shorten the body or sleeves, it is usually fairly straightforward to add (or omit) a few rows just below the armhole shaping on the body, or just below the sleeve-top shaping on a sleeve (page 70).

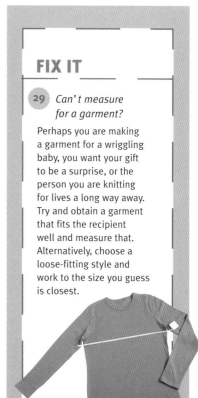

FIX IT

29 *Can't measure for a garment?*

Perhaps you are making a garment for a wriggling baby, you want your gift to be a surprise, or the person you are knitting for lives a long way away. Try and obtain a garment that fits the recipient well and measure that. Alternatively, choose a loose-fitting style and work to the size you guess is closest.

Typical ease for a sweater

Body measurement (BM)	Finished measurement (garment size)				
Bust/chest	Very close fit (BM minus 2in/5cm)	Close fit (= BM)	Standard fit (BM + 2in/5cm)	Loose fit (BM + 4in/10cm)	Very loose fit (BM + 6in/15cm or more)
32in/81cm	30in/76cm	32in/81cm	34in/86cm	36in/91cm	38in/97cm
34in/86cm	32in/81cm	34in/86cm	36in/91cm	38in/97cm	40in/102cm
36in/91cm	34in/86cm	36in/91cm	38in/97cm	40in/102cm	42in/107cm
38in/97cm	36in/91cm	38in/97cm	40in/102cm	42in/107cm	44in/112cm
40in/102cm	38in/97cm	40in/102cm	42in/107cm	44in/112cm	46in/117cm

30
Taking your measurements

If you want to measure yourself, ask someone to help. Use a tape measure and take your measurements over your normal underwear. Hold the tape around the body so it is neither tight nor loose. Make a note of each measurement.

31
Other measurements

You may need to take other body measurements, especially if you are adapting a design or designing your own pattern.

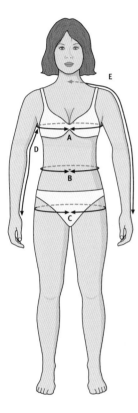

A: Bust or chest: Measure around the widest part.
B: Waist: Tie a length of string around your waist and settle it comfortably into place. This is your natural waistline. Measure along the line of the string but not too tightly.
C: Hips: Measure around the widest part.
D: Underarm length: With elbow slightly bent as shown, measure from 1in (2.5cm) below actual underarm down to narrowest part of wrist, just above hand.
E: Center back neck to wrist: Measure from the bone at the center back of the neck to the narrowest part of the wrist, just above the hand. (This measurement is sometimes used for drop-shoulder or batwing garments).

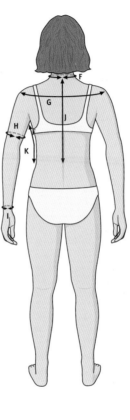

F: Neck measurement: Measure around the neck at the widest part. Note that the neck of a sweater must stretch sufficiently to fit easily over the head.
G: Back width: Measure across the back between the outer tips of the shoulder bones. This measurement is needed when calculating the instructions for a set-in sleeve garment.
H: Upper arm width: Measure around the upper arm at the widest point. Unless a tightly fitting sleeve is required, at least 1in (2.5cm) of ease is normally added to this measurement.
I: Wrist: Measure around the wrist, just above the hand. A cuff must stretch sufficiently to allow a closed fist to pass through.
J: Back neck to waist: Measure from the bone at the center back of the neck (the Atlas) down to the natural waistline. This measurement is normally taken to equal the measurement from the top of the shoulder down over the bust to the natural waistline, but in the case of a full bust a separate front measurement may be needed.
K: Waist to underarm: measure from the natural waistline to 1in (2.5cm) below the actual underarm. This measurement is used to calculate the body shaping for a fitted or semi-fitted garment.

32
Measuring for socks

To measure the length of the foot, stand upright in bare feet, with one foot on a sheet of paper. Use a pencil to mark the positions of the end of the big toe and the back of the heel. Measure between the marks. The leg length for socks is usually measured upward from the ankle, as shown. Instructions for socks are normally close-fitting, with no ease added to any measurements.

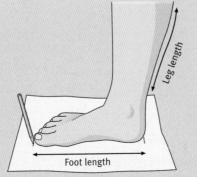

DESIGN

Learn how to select the garment styles and colors that will make you look your best, then how to adapt a knitting pattern, achieve a perfect fit, or even design your own garment from scratch.

Choosing colors

Learn about how colors work together and then try the color test (opposite) — in future you'll find it much easier to pick colors that will work for you.

33 Color theory

Designers in many fields use color theory and the color wheel to choose color schemes. Understanding color theory can help you choose colors that work well together and that therefore will help produce a successful knitted garment.

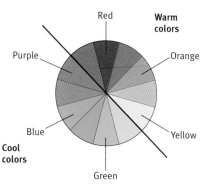

The color wheel

A rainbow of colors may be arranged in a circle like this, called a color wheel.

Primary colors: These are the pure hues of red, blue, and yellow. They cannot be made by mixing two colors together.

Secondary colors: These fall between the primary colors on the wheel: orange (made by mixing red and yellow); green (made by mixing yellow and blue); and purple (made by mixing blue and red).

Warm colors: From yellow through red to reddish purple, these colors form one-half of the color wheel. So a yellow that contains a certain amount of orange is called a warm yellow.

Cool colors: The other half of the color wheel, from purple through blue to green yellow, contains the cool colors. So a purple that contains a certain amount of blue is called a cool purple.

1. Complementary colors

Every color has a complementary color, which is directly opposite on the color wheel. For example, blue and orange are complementary colors, as are red and green, and yellow and purple. When complementary colors are used together, the sharp contrast between them produces a bright, lively effect on the eye.

2. Harmonious colors

Colors that are close to each other on the color wheel are called harmonious — blues and purples, or greens and blues for example. Using harmonious colors together produces a co-ordinated, restful effect.

3. Soft, bright colors

Softer colors are less intense than the true primary and secondary colors. Also shown here are some intermediate hues, for example turquoise, which sits on the color wheel between blue and green.

4. Pastel colors

Pastel colors, (sometimes called tints) are made by greatly reducing the intensity of a color, as a painter adds white to make a color paler.

5. Muted colors

These are correctly called tones and they include a proportion of the complementary color, so a muted green is made by adding a little red to green.

6. Neutral colors

The neutrals include creams, grays, and browns, and muted colors that are hard to describe such as brownish greens. A "warm" neutral, such as brown, contains more yellow or red, and a "cool" neutral, such as dove gray, contains more blue.

(34)

What color suits me?

The color you wear next to your face is the most important color to get right. Colors that suit you will enhance your skin tone and the colors of your hair and eyes, making you look bright-eyed and radiant; friends will say how well you look. Colors that don't suit you will make you look drained and tired.

We all have a favorite color, but this may not be the best color for us to wear. It isn't about what colors you like, it's about which colors like you!

Color test

Try this simple exercise, maybe with the help of a friend:

• Make a collection of as many different colors as you can find: balls of yarn from your stash, sweaters, scarves, T-shirts, etc. Take everything to a large mirror in good daylight. (When you stand before the mirror, the daylight should light your face, not the mirror).

• Hold each yarn in turn up to your face and study the effect. Do your eyes look bright or dull? Does your skin look healthy, or gray and shadowy? Sort the yarns and garments into two piles: good colors and bad colors.

• You should find that all the colors in the "good" pile have something in common. They will probably all fall within one third of the color wheel. They may also be mainly pastel, bright, dark, or muted. Other colors from the same area of the color wheel, in similar tints and tones, will probably suit you too.

• When you go shopping, make a point of wearing a top or a scarf that really suits you. Hold prospective purchases up to your face and look in a mirror to compare the effect.

• Don't keep clothes in colors that don't suit you. Dye them at home (see page 112), sell them, give them to charity, or swap them with friends.

These blues, purples, pinks, and grays are all cool colors, in mid to light tones.

These rusts, golds, and olive greens are warm colors, mainly in medium tones.

Bright, cheerful colors are great for vacations and weekends, but not necessarily suitable for the office.

FIX IT

35 *Favorite color doesn't suit you?*

Your favorite color is not necessarily the best color to wear next to your face, but that doesn't mean you can't wear it at all. If you really love orange, for example, but it doesn't suit you, you can knit yourself an orange purse or belt, (or buy orange shoes), but don't wear an orange scarf or sweater.

36 *Short height?*

Don't visually divide your body by wearing tops and bottoms in strongly contrasting colors or tones. However, you don't have to wear one color from top to toe—try wearing tone-on-tone. For example, a lavender sweater with a skirt in a muted tone of the same color will help you look taller.

37 *New hair color?*

If you re-color your hair, your skin tone and eye color remain the same. So if your new hair color suits you, colors that suited you before will still work for you.

If your hair is turning gray or white, again, your skin tone and eye color remain the same, so the same group of colors will still suit you. However, very bright colors and neutrals may make your skin look tired, so try using mid-tones of soft color to flatter mature skin.

All about drape

"Drape" is a term used to describe how soft and stretchy or stiff and firm a piece of knitting feels and how it falls around the body. The yarn you choose, the gauge, and the stitch construction will all have an effect on the drape of a finished piece.

Contrasting different drapes within the same garment can be very effective. Here, the fluffy silk and mohair ties, knitted in an elastic rib stitch, soften the neckline of a classic cardigan.

38 Soft, flexible knits

For shawls, wraps, scarves, or details such as a ruffled collar, you need a knitted fabric that drapes well. This is achieved by using one or more of the following:
• **Larger needles** than the recommended size to make the gauge looser. Suitable yarns are those that are slightly hairy, such as mohair or wool, so the stitches will not stretch out of shape.
• **Loosely spun lightweight yarns,** such as Shetland wool, to knit up a soft, delicate fabric.
• **Slippery yarns,** such as silk or viscose, or mixtures containing these fibers, which drape naturally because of their weight and smoothness. To avoid excess sagging, don't use larger needles than recommended.
• **Open stitch constructions,** such as lace stitches (page 88), which make fabrics that are light and flexible. Different lace stitch patterns will fall in different folds if gathered into ruffles.

39 Firm, stable knits

Some knits, such as structured jackets, pillow covers, and stuffed toys, require a stable fabric that will always keep its shape, without sagging or stretching. Such fabrics are constructed by using one or more of the following:
• **Smaller needles** than the recommended size, which makes the gauge tighter so the knit is firmer.
• **Tightly spun yarns,** which knit up into firm knitted fabrics.
• **Textured yarns,** such as bouclé wool, which discourage stitches from stretching so the knit retains its shape.
• **Solid-textured stitch patterns,** such as seed stitch (page 65), twists (page 90) and cables (page 90), which make firm knitting, with a tighter gauge than stockinette stitch.

40 Elastic knits

For a skinny-rib knit, or any part of a garment that needs to fit the body tightly, an elastic knit is required. When worn, the knitting is stretched to a greater or lesser degree, but when you take it off or wash it, it needs to return to its natural shape. Achieve this type of knitting by using:
• **Rib stitch** (page 64), or one of the many rib-stitch variations, normally worked on needles one or two sizes smaller than the size recommended for stockinette stitch.
• **Medium or tightly spun yarn with a high wool content** because wool fibers are naturally springy and elastic.

Texture

Texture adds an extra dimension to your knitting that is sometimes not fully appreciated. Texture can be matte, shiny, rough, knobbly, or smooth; it is not purely a visual quality, but also a quality you feel with your fingers and skin. Add texture to your work by choosing textured yarns or by using textured stitches.

41 Textured stitches

There are any number of textured stitches to choose from: ribs and rib variations, twists and cables (pages 90), bobbles and knots (pages 92), and many more. Choose plain, smooth yarns and light or bright colors to show off textured stitches. Textured yarns and dark colors will hide all but the heaviest of textures.

The relative firmness of the way the yarn is spun will affect the appearance of a stitch pattern: a tightly spun yarn will knit up into crisp, well-defined textured stitches, whereas a yarn with a looser spin will form softer, more gentle textured effects.

This highly textured cable-knit pillow stands out beautifully against the plain sofa, while the hand-made buttons, decorated with geometric dots, swirls, and lines, provide an eye-catching finishing touch.

42 Keep it light

A heavily textured knit will use more yarn than a plain knit in the same yarn, and will therefore weigh more, too. To avoid excess weight, which may cause a garment to stretch out of shape, choose lightweight, springy wool rather than heavier yarns such as cotton.

Nothing could be simpler to knit than rows of garter stitch, but varying both the yarn and the number of rows per stripe creates a one-of-a-kind piece with lots of different textures. Here, eyelash, feather, and mohair yarns are combined with ordinary worsted wool. This is also a great way of using up small amounts of yarn left over from other projects!

43 Textured yarns

The texture of yarns is derived either from the fiber itself or from the method by which it is spun. Various yarns spun in different ways to make different textures are shown on page 118. Choosing a yarn with an interesting texture, perhaps multi-colored or shade-dyed, is an easy way to transform a simple design into an extra-special garment.

Many textured yarns are best knitted in simple stitches, such as stockinette stitch or ribbing, or with very bold stitch patterns like big cables because the detail of more intricate stitches may be disguised by the yarn and the effect will be lost.

44 Make a contrast

To show off knits in luxurious textured yarns, wear them with plain, smooth fabrics: a mohair sweater with jeans, perhaps, or an angora wrap with a silk camisole.

Flattering your body shape

Are you tall and willowy, apple- or pear-shaped, or do you have an hourglass figure? Choose the style of your clothing carefully to enhance your good points and minimize any flaws.

45 Tall, slim figure

Bust: Small
Waist: Not well-defined
Hips: Slim
Legs: Slim and often long

Most clothes look great on you, but you should avoid styles that make you look too skinny and boyish. If you lack curves, the right choice of knitwear can help.

Shapes to choose

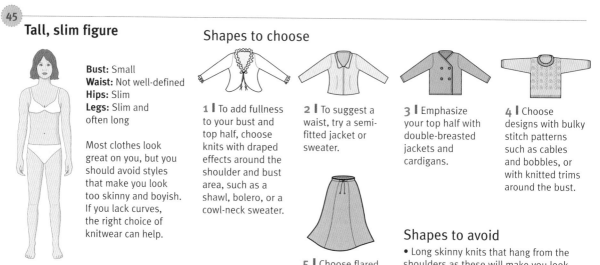

1 | To add fullness to your bust and top half, choose knits with draped effects around the shoulder and bust area, such as a shawl, bolero, or a cowl-neck sweater.

2 | To suggest a waist, try a semi-fitted jacket or sweater.

3 | Emphasize your top half with double-breasted jackets and cardigans.

4 | Choose designs with bulky stitch patterns such as cables and bobbles, or with knitted trims around the bust.

5 | Choose flared or A-line skirts to add curves to your hips.

Shapes to avoid

• Long skinny knits that hang from the shoulders as these will make you look like a beanpole.
• Pencil skirts.
• Belts at the waist as these will draw attention to your lack of waistline.

46 Apple-shaped figure

Bust: Average to full
Waist: Full
Hips: Slim in relation to bust
Legs: Usually slim

You need to choose styles to disguise—or divert attention from—your waist. Do this by making the most of your bust and slim hips, drawing the eye away from the tummy.

Shapes to choose

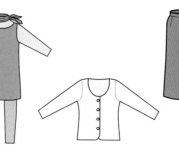

1 | Choose knitwear with patterns and details around the shoulders and bust, or accessorize this area with pretty jewelry or a scarf.

2 | If you are fairly tall, long tunics worn over slim-fitting pants, leggings, or skirts will skim over the problem waist area and emphasize your best points.

3 | Look for garments that skim the waistline without clinging.

4 | Choose straight, slim skirts and pants. Try flat-fronted pants, with a zipper fastening at the side or the back, to reduce tummy bulge.

Shapes to avoid

• Cropped tops—keep that tummy hidden.
• Full gathers or pleats around the waist because these add unnecessary bulk.
• Belts or other trims at the waist, which draw attention to the wrong area.

47 Pear-shaped figure

Bust: Small in relation to hips
Waist: Slim, often low (making a long-bodied shape)
Hips: Full
Legs: Often with heavy thighs

You need to balance your shape by minimizing the bottom half and emphasizing your bust and waist.

Shapes to avoid

• Tight, tapered pants (especially those with back pockets) or leggings as these will only emphasize wide hips.
• Big, baggy tops—these balance big hips, but the overall effect is just …big.
• Pants or skirts with bright patterns or bold details as these draw attention away from your upper body.

Shapes to choose

1 | Choose fitted or semi-fitted sweaters and jackets with stitch patterns or other decorative details at the neckline or in the shoulder/bust area.

2 | Flatter your slim waist by choosing a design that features a waist belt or ties but is not figure-hugging below the waist.

4 | Choose simple, A-line skirts and classic-cut pants that will not draw the eye to your lower body.

3 | Wear lighter-colored tops with skirts or pants in plain, dark colors.

48 Hourglass figure

Bust: Average to full
Waist: Slim
Hips: Average to full, only a little larger than bust
Legs: Curvaceous

Your shape is well-balanced, but some hourglass figures are fuller than others, and your legs may appear short.

Shapes to avoid

• Chunky, baggy knits as these add bulk all over.
• Breast pockets, which will make you look top-heavy.
• Wide-leg pants, or pants with lots of pockets or other details, which make your legs look shorter and heavier.

Shapes to choose

1 | Ribbed sweaters and fine, smooth knits that will make the most of your curvy shape.

2 | Sweaters and cardigans with fitted waists, deep waist ribs, or waist belts/ties, which will also flatter your body shape.

3 | High-waisted styles (empire-line), which fit beneath the bust (where the body is relatively slim), then flare out gently, giving the illusion of longer legs.

4 | Tailored clothing, which adds height. Choose a pencil skirt, or high-waisted pants.

FIX IT

49 *Narrow shoulders?*
Try a garment with cap sleeves, or set-in sleeves (page 69), perhaps with shoulder-pads (page 83), to add definition to the shoulder line.

50 *Broad shoulders?*
Try wearing garments with raglan sleeves (page 70), or cutaway armholes, to visually reduce the bulk in this area.

51 *Long upper body with short legs?*
Choose sweaters and jackets that finish no lower than 5in (12.5cm) below the waistline, and team them with a plain, dark skirt or pants to make the legs appear longer.

52 *Heavy upper arms?*
Choose long (or ¾ length) sleeves that do not fit tightly. A flared shape or a scalloped edge will make the arm appear relatively slim. Tight, short sleeves will make the arms look plumper.

53 *Large thighs?*
Boot-cut pants can balance large thighs. Or try wide-leg or straight-leg pants in a softly draping fabric; avoid unnecessary pockets.

54 *Short height?*
A sweater or jacket worn with a skirt or pants in a matching or toning color creates an illusion of height. Scalloped or chevron hems and asymmetrical shapes can help avoid strong lines that cut across the body. Also avoid horizontal stripes and wide contrasting belts.

Adapting knitting patterns

Sometimes you know what you want to make but can't find a printed pattern that's exactly right. Sometimes you like a sweater so much that you want to make another, but not an exact copy. Here's how to transform a basic design.

Designed by Martin Storey for Rowan, this simple sweater gives you ample scope to play around with the basic design. Why not try multi-colored stripes instead of the "zebra" stripes shown here, or alter the size of the stripes so that you have a mix of wide and narrow?

55 Changing the color

The simplest change you can make is to knit the sweater in a different color or colors. Choosing your own colorway makes a design unique to you. Buy the exact yarn specified in colors of your choice. Alternatively, you might choose several harmonious colors to knit simple stripes (page 26).

56 Changing the yarn

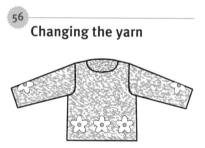

The sweater in the photograph is made in a pure cotton yarn, but you might prefer wool or perhaps a soft, fluffy yarn. Follow the guidelines for substituting yarns on page 16. If in doubt about the quantity of yarn you need, always buy extra.

57 Changing the edgings

You could substitute a few rows of garter stitch (page 49) or ribbing (using smaller needles), add frills (page 100), or work a crochet edging (page 138), perhaps in a contrasting color.

58 Changing the stitch or motif

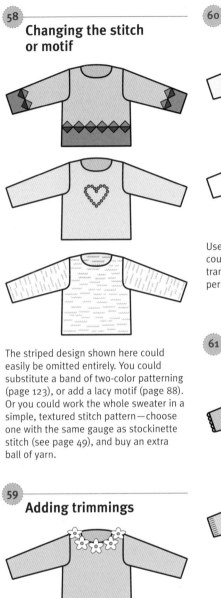

The striped design shown here could easily be omitted entirely. You could substitute a band of two-color patterning (page 123), or add a lacy motif (page 88). Or you could work the whole sweater in a simple, textured stitch pattern—choose one with the same gauge as stockinette stitch (see page 49), and buy an extra ball of yarn.

59 Adding trimmings

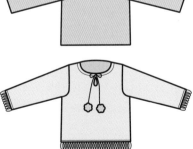

Change the balance of a sweater design by working a plain sweater and then adding knitted flowers (page 136) around the neckline. Or consider embellishing with pompoms, cords, tassels, or fringes, as described on page 132.

60 Adding embroidery

Use freestyle embroidery (page 128) or counted-stitch embroidery (page 126) to transform a plain sweater into a uniquely personal design.

61 Changing the neck detail

Instead of the simple semi-scoop neck in the photograph, you could work a rolled edge (page 72) or a collar (page 73). Or perhaps work the sweater front with a simple vertical slit, fastened with an interesting button at the neck. An extra ball of yarn may be required.

62 Adding pockets

Add patch or slit pockets wherever you want them, using one of the methods described on page 76. Extra yarn will be required.

63 Adjusting the length

The sweater in the photograph has no shaping between the lower edge and the beginning of the armhole shaping, making it easy to adjust the length of the body. You might prefer three-quarter sleeves or short sleeves.

Achieving perfect fit

You've taken your measurements accurately (page 25), chosen a flattering pattern (page 30), selected either the recommended yarn or a yarn of similar drape that knits to the same gauge (page 20), and bought your needles and other necessary accessories. Now there is just one more thing to do before you start knitting—make sure the item is going to fit.

64 Fitting guidelines

Run through the following checks to help get the best fit and to avoid or spot a fitting problem as early as possible:
• Check the measurements given in the pattern against your body measurements (page 25).
• Compare the measurements of each finished element, such as sleeve, front, and back, with a garment in your wardrobe of a similar style that you know fits you well. Will the body length suit you? Will the shoulder width be correct? If not, you may be able to make adjustments, as described opposite.

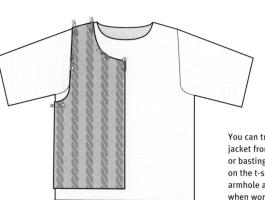

You can try a piece such as this jacket front for size, by pinning or basting it onto a t-shirt. Try on the t-shirt to see where the armhole and neckline will sit when worn.

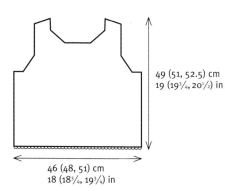

49 (51, 52.5) cm
19 (19³/₄, 20¹/₂) in

46 (48, 51) cm
18 (18³/₄, 19³/₄) in

• Check the measurements of each knitted piece as you complete it (page 21). If the measurements are incorrect, re-check your gauge. If your gauge is too tight or too loose, you will have to re-knit the piece. If your gauge is correct, maybe you have misread the instructions.
• Hold up or try on the pieces of the garment you are knitting as you complete them to check the size before you knit any more.

• Where a pattern instructs you to work to a certain length, make a note of the actual number of rows you work to obtain this length. Then when you work the matching piece (such as a second sleeve), work exactly the same number of rows. Another way is to work two matching pieces or two sides of a neckline at the same time, as shown on page 72.
• Always keep a record of any alterations you make to a pattern, in case you want to use the pattern again. To avoid spoiling a book, write on a photocopy of the pattern.
• Before assembling the garment pieces, block them (page 148), baste them together (page 147), and try on the garment. If you do need to unravel to make adjustments, at least you don't have to unpick finished seams.

65 To lengthen or shorten the body

Determine how much longer or shorter you want the garment to be. Adjust by working to a longer or shorter length before beginning the armhole shaping. Add or subtract the same number of rows on both front and back. If the garment is shaped at the waist, you must decide where to add (or omit) rows: above the waist, below the waist, or evenly spread above and below.

Adjust length here

66 To lengthen or shorten sleeves

This set-in sleeve begins at the wrist and increases gradually to the maximum width a short distance below armhole level. This usually enables you to complete the increasing and then work the sleeve to the exact length you want. If the garment is worked in a fancy stitch you may need to end on a particular pattern row.

Substantially shorter sleeve For a much shorter sleeve, such as a three-quarter sleeve beginning at the line A–A, calculate the number of rows that will need to be omitted from the sleeve length. Next, figure out how many stitches would have been increased over these missing rows, and add these extra stitches to the number given for casting on at the wrist. This is the number you should cast on for a sleeve that begins higher up the arm. Then increase the sleeve at the intervals given in the pattern, up to armhole level, and shape the top of the sleeve as given in the instructions.

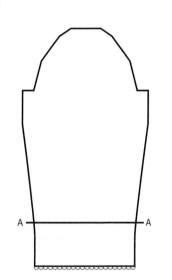

67 To make the body wider or narrower

Changing the width of a garment piece is trickier than changing the length, and is much easier to plan if the garment is made in a plain stitch.

• Calculate the number of stitches to be added or omitted to make the width you need, and divide them evenly between the front and back of the garment. For example, if you want to add 12 stitches to the body of a sweater, you should add 6 stitches to the front and 6 stitches to the back.

• After shaping the armholes as given in the pattern, the total number of stitches remaining will include 6 extra stitches.

• Spread the extra stitches evenly across the shoulder and neck shapings: in our example, you would add 2 stitches to each shoulder, and 2 stitches to the front neck, (on the back, 2 stitches to each shoulder and 2 stitches to the back neck).

Garments in fancy all-over stitches, those with raglan sleeves or complicated neck shapings, can be difficult to adjust widthwise. To avoid unforeseen complications, chart the pieces stitch by stitch on graph paper (page 39).

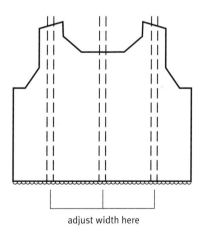

adjust width here

⊚TRY IT

68 Knit it again

Now that you've made a sweater or jacket that fits you perfectly, you can use the same basic pattern to make another one, making the changes by using one or more of the methods described on page 32.

FIX IT

69 *Shoulders too wide?*

Shoulder seams that are too wide or stretchy can be firmed up with a tightly worked row of crochet (page 144). If you have narrow shoulders, try adding some shoulder pads (see page 83).

70 *Neckband too tight?*

Loosen a bound-off edge by binding it off with a needle one or two sizes larger. If the neckband is worked by picking up stitches from a bound-off neckline, unravel the binding-off and pick up the stitches directly from the neckline stitches.

71 *Neckline too loose?*

Try working a tight row of single crochet across the back neck edge, below the neckband or collar, or right across from shoulder to shoulder (page 144).

Basic design principles

The basis of all design calculation is the gauge sample. Once you know the number of stitches and rows to 4in (10cm), you can use simple math to figure out the numbers of stitches and rows required for a piece of knitting of any shape or size. Start with a straightforward shape, such as a scarf or shawl. More complex shapes are shown on pages 38–39.

72

Simple rectangles

A long scarf is usually about 7–10in (17.5–25cm) wide, and may be any length from 40–60in (100–150cm) or more. Think about the properties you want in a scarf: warm, lightweight, and flexible. Remember also that a scarf does not usually have a "wrong" side—it needs to look equally good on both sides, although not exactly the same.

1 Choose a suitable yarn and try a few stitches using the needle size recommended on the ball band: the simplest reversible stitch is garter stitch (page 49). Alternatively, try various ribs (page 64). Keep a note of the needles and stitches you use. Choose the stitch you like best then count the stitches and rows to 4in (10cm) to find the gauge (see page 20).

2 Decide on suitable measurements and sketch them roughly. Suppose you want a scarf 8in (20cm) wide and about 48in (120cm) long, and your gauge is 18 stitches and 24 rows to 4in (10cm).

Working in inches: Number of stitches per inch is 18/4 = 4.5; number of rows per inch is 24/4 = 6. So for a width of 8in, you need 8 x 4.5 = 36 stitches; and for a length of 48in you need 48 x 6 = 288 rows.

Working in centimeters: Number of stitches per cm = 18/10 = 1.8; number of rows per cm = 24/10 = 2.4. For a width of 20cm you need 20 x 1.8 = 36 sts; and for a length of 120cm you need 120 x 2.4 = 288 rows.

Write your calculated stitches and rows on your drawing for easy reference.

48in (120cm) = 288 rows

8in (20cm)
= 36 stitches

3 Now you can figure out how much yarn you need, as described on page 17. To knit the scarf, just follow your diagram—there's no need to write the instructions out in words.

73 Simple triangles

Garments other than scarves usually require some form of shaping. A simple example is a triangular shawl, worked from the point up to the long edge, increasing at regular intervals at both side edges.

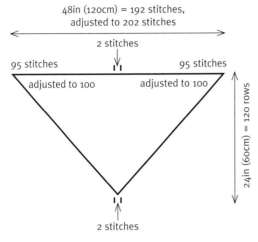

48in (120cm) = 192 stitches, adjusted to 202 stitches

2 stitches

95 stitches — adjusted to 100

95 stitches — adjusted to 100

24in (60cm) = 120 rows

2 stitches

1 | Make a gauge sample as in step 1, opposite, and count the gauge. Draw a rough diagram of the size you want. Referring to step 2, opposite, calculate the number of stitches along the top edge, and the number of rows from the point to the top edge (measured straight, not along the sloping edge). Mark these on your diagram.

The sides of a triangular shawl usually slope at about 45 degrees. Suppose your gauge is 16 stitches and 20 rows to 4in (10cm). To increase from 2 stitches at the point to 192 stitches along the top edge, you need to increase 190 stitches over 120 rows. Remember, you will be increasing at both side edges—95 stitches on each side. Divide the number of rows by the number of stitches to be

increased at each side: 120/95 = 24/19, a very awkward figure. However, by rounding the figures up or down, you can come up with a much simpler fraction: 120/100 = 12/10 = 6/5. For every 6 rows, you need to increase 5 stitches at each side. This method would be easy to follow in a stitch pattern with a repeat of 6 or 12 rows. The shawl would be 10 stitches wider than you planned across the top edge—not crucial for a shawl.

Write your new figures for the stitches and rows onto the diagram. Write down a reminder of how you are going to work the increasing: in this case, "Increase 1 stitch at each end of 1st, 2nd, 3rd, 4th, and 5th rows. Work 1 row without shaping. Repeat these 6 rows."

Rounding up or down

You may need to round the stitches and/or rows up or down to fit a particular stitch pattern.

Suppose your stitch pattern requires a multiple of 6 stitches plus 3, and you also want to add 4 selvage stitches (see page 60). In our example scarf, you could change the width to 37 stitches (5 sets of 6 stitches plus 3, plus 4 for the selvage).

Suppose your stitch pattern repeats over 14 rows. You can round the length up to 294 rows (21 sets of 14 rows) or down to 280 (20 sets of 14 rows), whichever you prefer.

101 stitches

120 rows

2 | You now need to calculate how much yarn you need. You can see that this triangular shape is the equivalent of a rectangle of 101 stitches x 120 rows. Use the method on page 17 to figure out the yarn requirement.

74 Working from the long edge

Some stitch patterns are difficult to follow when increasing at the edges. It may be easier to work a shawl in such a stitch by starting at the long top edge, and decreasing down to the point because that way you can see where you are in the stitch pattern.

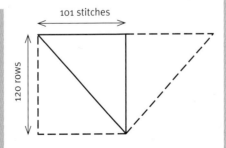

This shawl is worked in mohair yarn in garter stitch with "yarn over" increasing (page 54) and a twisted fringe added (page 135).

◉TRY IT

75 **Scarf variations**

• Try knitting a long scarf in the other direction, from end to end instead of from side to side.

• Make a multi-stripe scarf using lots of odds and ends from your yarn stash: just make sure the yarns you choose knit to a similar gauge (see pages 20 and 118). It doesn't matter if the row gauge differs, but the width gauge should match throughout.

• Add different trimmings to change the look: tassels, fringes, pompoms, crochet edges, and so on are great fun.

Schematics and graphs

Simple garment pieces may be planned in the same way as a scarf or shawl, with the aid of schematic drawings. More complicated shapes can be planned in detail on graph paper. As always, start with a gauge sample using your chosen yarn, stitch, and needles.

76 Simple garment pieces

A basic garment in a simple stitch is quite straightforward to plan. Here's how you might plan a sweater with square armholes.

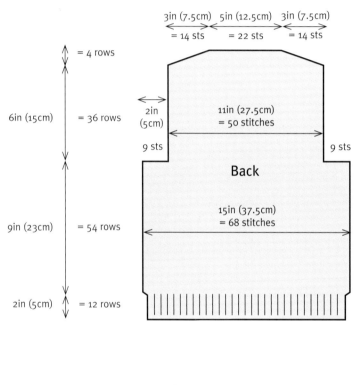

Back

1 ▎ Suppose your main gauge is 18 stitches and 24 rows to 4in (10cm). Decide on the measurements you need (see page 25), including an amount for ease (page24). Make a rough drawing of the shape of each piece and write the measurements on it. Translate each measurement into stitches or rows then round the numbers of stitches up or down to suit your stitch pattern. Make the numbers of rows into even numbers.

For the square armholes shown, 2in (5cm) deep, you need to bind off 9 stitches at each edge to reduce the width from 68 to 50 stitches. Divide the top edge into three parts, the central section equal to the width required across the back neck. The two shoulder sections may be sloping, as shown, in two or three steps (over four or six rows).

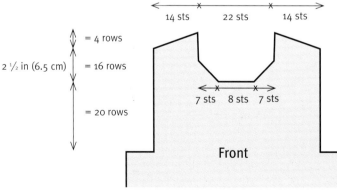

Front

2 ▎ On this sweater the front is the same as the back except for the front neck shaping, which may be any depth required as long as it will stretch over the head. Draw in the shape of the front neckline, with a measurement for the depth translated into an even number of rows. Divide the front neckline into approximate thirds. The stitch groups at either side will be decreased over the next few rows, and the remaining center group will be placed on a stitch holder or bound off.

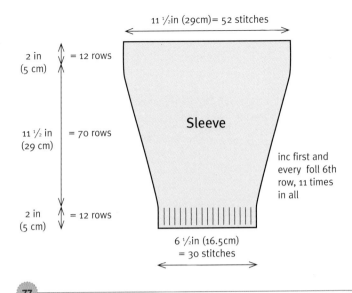

11 ½ in (29cm)= 52 stitches

2 in (5 cm) = 12 rows

11 ½ in (29 cm) = 70 rows

Sleeve

inc first and every foll 6th row, 11 times in all

2 in (5 cm) = 12 rows

6 ½ in (16.5cm) = 30 stitches

Sleeve

3 | The width across the top of a drop-shoulder sleeve should be twice the depth of the armhole minus ½in (1.2cm) so the sleeve top is slightly stretched and will not pucker. Add extra length to the underarm measurement to allow for stitching the top few rows to the armhole shaping. Check that half the width across the top of the back, plus the whole sleeve length (including the extra rows), equals the body measurement from center back neck to wrist (see page 25), and adjust the sleeve length if necessary.

The sleeve shown needs to increase from 30 stitches after the ribbing at the wrist to 52 stitches, an increase of 22 stitches (11 on each side). Divide the number of rows by the number of increases on each side: 70/11 = 6, with 4 rows remaining. So you should increase 1 stitch at each end of the first and every following 6th row, 11 times in all, then work without shaping to 70 rows from the top of the ribbing; add 12 more rows to fit into the square armhole.

77

Complicated shaping

Sometimes it is better to draw a specific diagram using graph paper. For example, if you want to work a raglan sleeve or armhole, it can be tricky to juggle the numbers of stitches and rows to match the measurements you want.

Each graph-paper square represents one stitch. Special knitters' graph paper has "squares" that are actually rectangles, representing the proportions of the average knitted stitch (shorter and wider than a true square). Draw the outline of each piece on the graph paper in pencil.

The raglan shaping of the armholes and sleeves should take up the same number of rows. Here, the raglan armholes on the back and front each begin by binding off 4 stitches at each side (over two consecutive

rows), and then decrease on alternate rows. On the sleeve more stitches need to be decreased within the same number of rows, so toward the top decreases are placed on every row.

On the front (right front shown here), the raglan shaping matches the back, but the V-neck requires a different slope: 8 stitches to decrease over 28 rows. So the steps are each 3 rows deep, with a few extra rows at the top.

When you are sure you have all the details correct, draw over your outlines with a fine pen and erase the pencil marks. Graphs like these can also be used to indicate stitch patterns, color changes, and other details of the design.

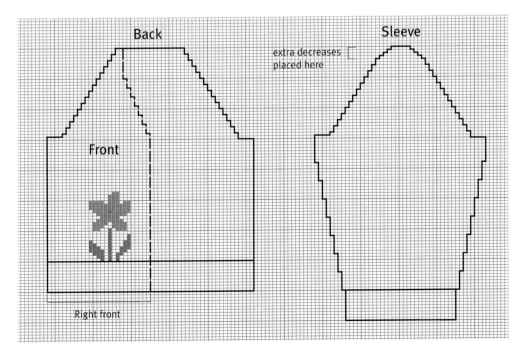

Back

Sleeve

extra decreases placed here

Front

Right front

Putting it all together

Sometimes you see a lovely new yarn that immediately suggests "evening wrap" or "baby blanket." Perhaps you want to make a gift for a family member or friend, so you need to consider what they would like (and how much time you have): a scarf or a sweater? Maybe you just want to knit something in an intriguing stitch you have come across elsewhere. Designing your own project can be confusing, so here's a checklist to make sure you've thought of everything.

78

Design checklist

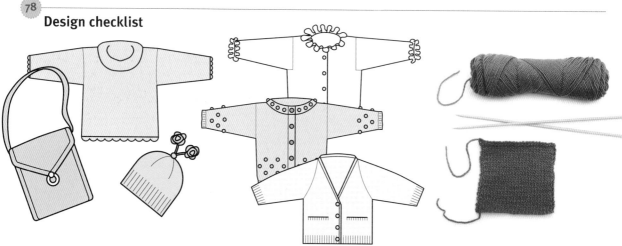

1 | Choose what you want to make: sweater, jacket, scarf, hat, blanket, babywear, purse, and so on. Select a suitable yarn: consider warmth, drape, washability, price, and availability. Decide on the color(s) you want. Sketch some ideas.

2 | Think about the texture and how different stitches behave, for example on ribbing and hems (page 64). Decide on the details: what type of borders (page 95), what type of sleeves (page 68), what collar (page 72) or pockets (page 76), what stitch pattern(s) or motif(s).

3 | If possible, buy just one ball of yarn; if this is not possible, consult commercial patterns for similar garments as a rough guide to quantity. Make one or more gauge sample(s) as described on page 20. Decide on the needle size(s) you will use. Count the gauge for your chosen needle size(s), stitch(es) and yarn(s).

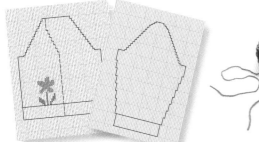

4 | Decide on the measurements of your project and make a rough sketch of all the main pieces. Translate the gauge into stitches and rows. For tricky shapes, use the graph-paper method (explained in detail on page 39). Try to think through the construction of each piece so you know exactly what you intend to do.

5 | Estimate the total amount of yarn you need (as on page 17). If you need to buy more yarn, buy it now. (Never start a project with insufficient yarn in case it gets discontinued).

6 | For a garment, you can begin with any piece: try making the back first (because it is probably the simplest shape), and check that the measurements match your schematic drawing. You can also check garment pieces on the body.

7 ❙ Now make one sleeve. The back and one sleeve should use about half your yarn. Fold the sleeve in half to check the fit with the armhole shaping. Adjust the sleeve-head shaping, if needed.

8 ❙ Now knit the other pieces in any order you choose. Assemble the garment as explained on pages 140–147 and knit on any neckband, front bands, etc., as required. Block the garment (page 148) and sew on buttons, work embroidery, and so on.

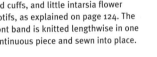

This V-neck baby jacket in Aran- weight yarn has raglan sleeves, ribbed welts and cuffs, and little intarsia flower motifs, as explained on page 124. The front band is knitted lengthwise in one continuous piece and sewn into place.

79
Start simple

If you have never designed your own project before, start with something simple in a bulky yarn for quick results. It's better to succeed with a simple idea than to start something complicated, get tied up in lots of calculations and unforeseen problems, and end by abandoning the project. Once you have successfully completed a couple of simple, quick-to-knit projects, you'll be ready to tackle something more challenging.

80
Buy plenty of yarn

If in doubt, buy extra yarn—you can always make a hat with what's left.

BASIC TECHNIQUES

From casting on, through knitting, purling, binding off, joining yarns, and working shapings, this chapter describes in detail the basic skills any knitter needs to know.

Preparing yarn

Many yarns are now supplied in balls that may be pulled out from the center so the ball won't roll away from you as you knit. However, some yarns, especially hand-dyed yarns, come in hanks. If you don't want to end up in knots when knitting, you will need to wind the hank into a ball.

Winding a center-pull ball from a hank

If you have purchased yarn on a hank, or have wound it into a hank for dyeing (see page 112) you will need to wind it into a ball before you can knit. A ball that may be pulled out from the center is most convenient.

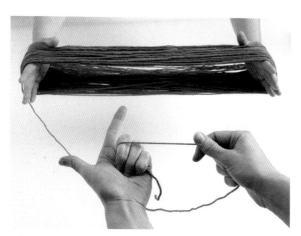

1 I Untwist the hank and remove any knotted ties. Stretch it taut between a friend's hands or across the back of a chair. Hold the tail of the yarn tightly beneath three fingers of your left hand.

2 I Hold your left thumb and index finger at right angles and wind the yarn around them in a figure eight about ten times.

3 I Bring the two halves of the figure eight together, off your index finger, but keep your thumb at the center, on top of the starting tail.

4 I Keep your thumb at the center throughout. Wind the yarn around and around to form a ball, changing position slightly as the ball grows, to make an even shape. The finished ball unwinds easily from the center.

These balls can both be pulled from the center.

Casting on

The various methods of casting on give different results, suitable for different purposes. Some have more stretch, for example. Try them out to see and feel the difference. In all cases, the tail ends can be used for sewing up seams or darned in unobtrusively (see page 143).

82 Making a slip knot

Every piece of knitting begins with a slip knot.

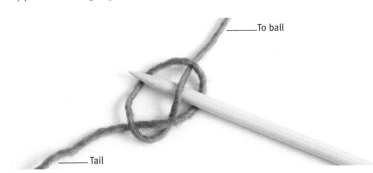

To ball

Tail

Loop the yarn in the direction shown, leaving a tail of desired length (see below). Use the needle tip to catch the yarn inside the loop. Tighten the knot gently on the needle.

⊚TRY IT

84 Get comfortable

To try out any basic technique, choose a medium-weight, smooth yarn (worsted or Aran weights are good for beginners) and a pair of needles of the size recommended on the ball band (page 16). Sit in a comfortable chair that will not restrict your arm movements. A light source over your left shoulder (if you are right handed) is very helpful.

83 Working the long-tail cast on

This method makes a firm, elastic edge that will not stretch out of shape. It is also called the German or single-needle method.

2 **|** Slide the needle up through the loop on your thumb and then use your right index finger to carry the main yarn counter-clockwise around the needle tip, as shown.

3 **|** Draw the new loop through the loop on your thumb, making a new stitch on the needle. Allow the loop to drop from your thumb and pull up the end so the stitch sits snugly but not tightly on the needle.

1 **|** Begin with a slip knot, leaving a long tail of yarn, about three times the length of the cast-on edge to be made. Hold the needle in your right hand. Loop the tail around your left thumb, and hold the yarn leading to the ball in your right hand, as shown for the English method on page 46.

4 **|** Repeat the steps until you have the required number of stitches, including that first slip-knot stitch in your count. The stitches should slide along the needle quite easily and be evenly spaced.

Working the cable cast on

Like long-tail cast on, this method makes a firm, elastic edge that will not stretch out of shape. It is also called the two-needle method.

1 **I** Make a slip knot with a tail about 6in (15cm) long. Hold the needle with the knot in your left hand (if you are right-handed). This is the first stitch. Insert the right needle into the knot from front to back, as shown.

2 **I** Wrap the yarn around the right needle tip, counter-clockwise.

3 **I** Draw the new loop down through the stitch on both needles and pull it through, keeping the first stitch on the left needle.

4 **I** Pass the left needle through the new loop from right to left, and slip the loop from the right needle onto the left needle. This is the second stitch.

5 I Insert the right needle between the two stitches from front to back (not through the new stitch) and wrap the yarn as before.

6 I Draw this new loop through and slip it onto the left needle as before, making a third stitch. Repeat step 5 until you have the required number of stitches.

86

Working the simple thumb cast on

This makes a loose, non-bulky edge of single loops, especially useful to make an edge which will be joined into a seam, or where stitches will later be picked up (page 62). It is often used within the body of the knitting to add a group of extra stitches. Otherwise, begin with a slip knot with a short tail, as here.

1 I Loop the working yarn around your right thumb as shown. Hold the needle in your left hand.

2 I Slide the loop onto the needle tip.

3 I Repeat until you have the required number of stitches. Do not make the loops too tight.

Holding the yarn and needles

There are several ways to hold the yarn and needles, derived from knitting traditions from different parts of the world. Two common methods are shown here, together with a method for left-handers. Whatever method you use, the yarn should flow freely through your fingers, and the resulting stitches should be of a consistent size.

87

Preparing to work the English method

This method is commonly used in England and the US. The yarn is controlled by the right hand.

Alternatively, you can hold the right-hand needle in the way you hold a pen.

1 Hold the needle with the stitches in your left hand and tension the yarn by winding it around the fingers of your right hand, as shown.

2 Pick up the working needle with your right hand, in the way you would hold a table knife. Your right index finger controls the yarn.

88

Preparing to work the Continental method

This method is favored in the main areas of Europe. The yarn is controlled by the left hand.

1 Hold the needle with the stitches in your right hand and wrap the yarn around the fingers of your left hand.

2 Pass the needle with the stitches to your left hand and pick up the working needle with your right hand. Your left index finger controls the yarn.

89

Preparing to work the left-handed method

Left-handers may find this method easier. The yarn is controlled in the left hand and the stitches to be worked are held on the right-hand needle.

1 Hold the needle with the stitches in your right hand and wind the yarn around the fingers of your left hand as for the Continental method.

2 Pick up the working needle with your left hand. Your left index finger controls the yarn.

Working knit stitch

Pick up your needles and tension the yarn as shown opposite for the method you wish to use. Now you are ready to knit. The first stitch to be worked into should be about ½–¾in (1.5–2cm) from the needle tip. Hold the yarn at the back of the work, behind the needles.

90
Knitting with the English method

In the UK and America this is the method most knitters are familiar with.

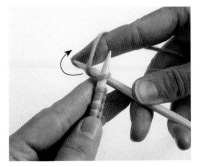

1 Insert the right needle tip from left to right (front through to back) into the first stitch. Wrap the yarn under and then over the right needle tip, as shown.

2 Pull the new loop through, allowing the stitch to drop from the left needle and making a new stitch on the right needle. Continue across the row in the same way or for as long as the pattern requires. When you reach then end, turn the work around to begin the next row.

91
Knitting with the Continental method

On the main areas of the Continent this is the favored method of knitting. Once mastered, it can be considerably quicker than the English method.

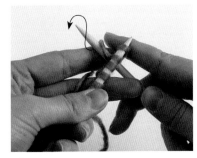

1 Insert the right needle through the first stitch from left to right (front through to back) and lay the yarn across the tip.

2 Use the right needle tip to pull the new loop through, steadying the loop with your right index finger, if necessary. Allow the old stitch to drop from the left needle. Continue across the row in the same way or for as long as the pattern requires. When you reach the end, turn the work around to begin the next row.

92
Knitting with the left-handed method

Left-handers may find this method easier to master than the previous two. Right-handers may also find this method useful as it makes it possible to knit back across a row without turning, which is useful when making bobbles (page 93) or when the work is very heavy or cumbersome.

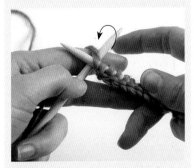

1 Insert the left needle tip through the first stitch from left to right (front through to back). Wrap the yarn under and over the left needle tip, as shown.

2 Pull the new loop forward through the stitch, making a new stitch on the left needle and allowing the old stitch to drop from the right needle. Continue across the row in the same way or for as long as the pattern requires. When you reach then end, turn the work around to begin the next row.

Working purl stitch

Purl stitch is the second basic knitting stitch you need to learn. Together with the knit stitch, purl forms the basis of all other knitting patterns. For purling, the yarn is held at the front of the work, in front of the needles.

93

Purling with the English method

If you knit with the English method this is how to purl.

1 | Insert the right needle tip into the first stitch on the left needle from right to left (back through to front). Wrap the yarn counter-clockwise around the right needle tip, as shown.

2 | Carry the new loop backward through the stitch to make a new stitch on the right needle, allowing the old stitch to drop off the left needle. Repeat as required.

94

Purling with the Continental method

If you knit with the Continental method, this is how to purl.

1 | Insert the right needle from right to left (back through to front) into the first stitch and lay the yarn counter-clockwise over the needle tip, as shown, pulling it downward with your left index finger.

2 | Use the right needle tip to carry the new loop back through the stitch, making a new stitch on the right needle and allowing the old stitch to drop from the left needle. Repeat as required.

95

Purling with the left-handed method

Follow this method to purl if you have learned to knit using the left-handed method.

1 | Insert the left needle into the first stitch from back through to front and wrap the yarn around it clockwise.

2 | Draw the new loop through the stitch, making a new stitch on the left needle and allowing the old stitch to drop from the right needle. Repeat as required.

Working basic knit and purl stitch patterns

When you knit, the bump of the old stitch is left at the back of the work, away from you, while when you purl, the bump of the old stitch falls to the front of the work, toward you. By combining knit and purl stitches you can create a huge range of stitch patterns. Here are a few basic patterns to begin with.

96

Basic stitches

Garter stitch

When you knit every row, the bumps of the stitches form in rows alternately on the front and back of the work. Garter stitch looks the same from both sides.
Suits any number of stitches.
Row 1: K to end.
Repeat this row.

Stockinette stitch

The right side (knit side) of stockinette stitch is smooth, while the back (purl side) is bumpy.
Suits any number of stitches.
Row 1: K to end.
Row 2: P to end.
Repeat these 2 rows.

Reverse stockinette stitch

The purl side (wrong side) of stockinette stitch shows all the bumps of the stitches.
Suits any number of stitches.
Row 1: P to end.
Row 2 K to end.

Caterpillar stitch

Groups of purl stitches on the right side of stockinette stitch form little rows of bumps.
Requires a multiple of 8 stitches, plus 1.
Row 1: K to end.
Row 2: P to end.
Row 3: K2, * P5, K3, * repeat from * to * to the last 7 stitches, P5, K2.
Row 4: P to end.
Rows 5 and 6: as rows 1 and 2.
Row 7: P3, * K3, P5, * repeat from * to * to last 6 sts, P3, K3.
Row 8: P to end.
Repeat these 8 rows.

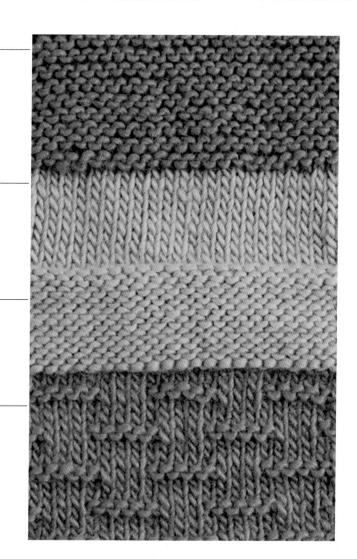

Binding off

Binding off links the stitches together at the end of a piece of knitting so that they will not unravel. Stitches may be bound off knitwise or purlwise, to suit the stitch pattern used. When shaping a garment you will sometimes be required to bind off (cast off) some stitches and continue working on others.

97 Binding off knitwise

This is the usual method of binding off. It is worked with the right side of stockinette stitch facing you and makes a neat edge.

1 | Knit the first two stitches to be bound off in the usual way.

2 | Use the left needle tip to lift the first stitch over the second and off the right needle, as shown.

3 | Knit the next stitch and repeat. If you are binding off all the stitches, you will be left with one last stitch on the right needle. Cut the yarn leaving a 6in (15cm) tail and pull it through the last loop.

FIX IT

100 Bound-off edge too tight?

The bound-off edge should stretch as much as the knitting. This is especially important at a neck edge. To ensure that the edge is not too tight, change to a needle one or two sizes larger to work the bind-off.

101 Not sure how to count?

If you are only binding off a certain number of stitches (e.g. to begin an armhole shaping), count the stitches as you lift them over and off, not as you knit them. The single stitch remaining on the right needle after binding off the group counts as the first stitch of the next row.

98 Binding off purlwise

Sometimes you may need to bind off purlwise, as on a wrong side row of stockinette stitch.

Purl the first two stitches to be bound off. With the yarn at the front of the work, insert the left needle through the back of the first stitch to lift it over the second and off the right needle. Repeat as required.

99 Binding off in rib

When binding off a rib or other stitch pattern, work each stitch as knit or purl according to the pattern to make a neat, elastic edge.

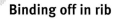

Referring to the instructions above, bind off the knit stitches knitwise and the purl stitches purlwise.

Fixing mistakes

If you drop a stitch, or notice a mistake in your knitting, don't leave it until later, fix it straight away, before knitting any further.

102 Picking up a dropped stitch

Even skillful knitters drop stitches sometimes. Take the knitting to the point directly above the dropped stitch and correct the error as explained here.

1 | On the knit side of stockinette stitch, use a crochet hook to pick up the loop at the bottom of the ladder. Catch the bar of yarn that slipped out of this loop, and draw it through the loop on the hook.

2 | Repeat the process to the top of the ladder. Slip the loop back onto the left needle without twisting it.

103 Correcting a mistake a few stitches back

If you haven't gone very far beyond a mistake, the easiest method of correcting it is to unpick your stitches back to the error and then continue knitting from there. Here's how.

1 | This ribbing has a wrong stitch four stitches back along the right needle (circled). Insert the tip of the left needle into the stitch below the first stitch on the right needle, from front to back.

2 | Slip the stitch off the right needle and pull gently on the yarn to unravel the loop. Repeat as required until you have unraveled the wrong stitch. Re-knit the stitches correctly.

104 Correcting a mistake a few rows below

Sometimes you won't notice a mistake until you have completed a few rows. It isn't necessary to unpick your work all the way back to the error.

1 | This knitting has a mistake five rows below the needles, (circled). Work along the row up to the required stitch column and drop the stitch off the needle.

2 | Gently stretch the knitting to ladder it down to (and including) the mistake. Use a crochet hook to re-work the stitches up to the needle in the same way as for a dropped stitch.

105 Correcting bigger mistakes

Sometimes you will need to unravel whole rows of knitting and put the stitches back on the needles.

1 | Slip the knitting off the needles and carefully pull on the yarn to unravel each row in turn, down to one row above the row you want to put back on the needles.

2 | Hold the work in your left hand and a smaller-size needle in your right (if you are right-handed). Insert the needle purlwise (as if to purl, see page 48) through the first stitch of the row you want, then pull the loop of yarn out of the stitch. Repeat along the row. When you re-start the knitting, change to the correct needle size and watch out for any stitches that may be twisted: use the needle tips to slip them back and forth to the correct position.

Joining yarns

Sometimes you run out of yarn and need to join in a new ball; sometimes the pattern requires that you change to another color. Usually this is best done at the beginning of a row but it may be necessary to make the join in the middle of a row. Here's how to do both.

FIX IT

106 *Worried about running out of yarn mid row?*

A row of knitting normally uses a length of yarn about 2 ½ times the width of the piece (laid flat). When you think you have enough yarn left for two rows, double the yarn to find the center and tie a loose knot there. Continue knitting: if you complete one row before reaching the knot, you have enough yarn left for another row. (Untie the knot when you reach it).

107

Joining yarn at the beginning of a row

The best place to join in a new ball of yarn is at the beginning of a row so the tails can be run in along the seam.

At the beginning of a row, tie the new yarn around the old yarn tail with a simple knot and slide the knot up close to the needle. Continue with the new yarn. Before joining the seam, unpick the knot to keep the seam smooth. Even out any loose stitches and run in the yarn tails along the seam (long tails can be used to join a seam).

108

Joining yarn in the middle of a row

Sometimes you can't avoid joining yarn in the middle of a row and, in fact, it is inevitable when working circular knitting, though you may still prefer to make the change in a discreet area such as at the underarm of a sweater.

1 | Leaving tails of at least 6in (15cm), tie the new yarn around the old yarn with a simple knot and slide the knot up close to the needles. Continue knitting with the new yarn.

2 | When the knitting is complete, unpick the knot. On the wrong side, run in the right-hand tail along the back of the row to the left, and the left-hand tail along to the right, for six to eight stitches in each direction. Use a tapestry needle for this, weaving the yarn through adjacent stitches, as shown.

3 | If the yarn is bulky, you can reduce the thickness of each tail. Untwist the tail and snip away half the strands, quite close to the work. Then run in the reduced tails.

Striped patterns

Knitting stripes is one of the easiest ways to add color to your design, especially if you position your color changes so that you don't have to keep cutting and rejoining the different colored yarns. Stripes are often worked in stockinette stitch but they can be combined successfully with ribs and textured designs.

109 Working stripes over even numbers of rows

If each stripe in the sequence has an even number of rows, you can carry the colors up the side edge of the knitting because each color will start and finish on the same edge of the work.

To carry a color up the side edge of just two rows, bring the new color up behind the old color to begin the next stripe. This makes a neat edge with the carried loops at the back of the work.

To carry a color up the side edge of four or more rows, twist the colors at the side edge on every other row to prevent large, loose loops.

110 Working one-row stripes in three colors

One-row stripes using three colors (or any odd number of colors) may be worked without cutting and re-joining yarns. Each yarn will be carried alternately up one side and then the other.

Row 1: Using A, K to end.
Row 2: Using B, P to end.
Row 3: Using C, K to end.
Continue in stockinette stitch (beginning with a P row), using the colors A, B, and C in sequence. At the end of each row, the next color to use is waiting for you.

111 Working ridge stripes

Using A, work 4 rows stockinette stitch.
Using B, work 2 rows garter stitch.
Repeat these 6 rows, carrying the colors up the side edge as left.

112 Working ribbed stripes

Varying the stitch pattern can make interesting stripes.

Work in K2, P2 rib as explained on page 64.
Using A, work 4 rows.
Using B, work 4 rows.
Repeat these 8 rows.

Increasing

Increasing makes extra stitches to shape the knitting, or it can be used within textured or lace stitch patterns, when each increase is normally balanced by a corresponding decrease (pages 56–59). There are four main ways to work increases: yarn over, knit twice in the same stitch, make one, or make one through the back loop.

113

Increase methods

The basic increase methods are yarn over; knit twice into the same stitch; make one, and make one through the back loop. Your choice will depend on whether or not you wish to make a feature of the increase and whether you wish to create an eyelet.

Yarn over (yo or Yo)

This method creates a visible hole (an eyelet) in the knitting. Depending on the stitch pattern in use, yarn over may be worked in one of four ways.

Knit twice into the same stitch (ktw or Ktw)

This method makes a firm increase. It is best worked at the edge of a piece where it will be disguised by a seam because it is not particularly neat.

Working yarn over between two knit stitches

Bring the yarn forward between the needle tips and back over the top of the right-hand needle, ready to knit the next stitch.

Working yarn over between two purl stitches

Take the yarn over the top of the right-hand needle to the back then bring it forward between the needle tips into position to purl the next stitch.

1 Knit into the stitch in the usual way but leave the stitch on the left needle. Insert the needle through the back of the same stitch.

Working yarn over between a knit and purl stitch

Bring the yarn forward between the needle tips then back over the top of the right-hand needle. Bring it forward again between the needle tips, ready to purl the next stitch.

Working yarn over between a purl and a knit stitch

Take the yarn over the top of the right needle to the back of the work, ready to knit the next stitch.

2 Wrap the yarn again and knit another stitch, allowing the old stitch to slip from the left needle.

Double yarn over (yo tw or Yotw)

This increase is mainly used in lace patterns when an extra-large hole is required. Within a stitch pattern, it may be balanced by two corresponding decreases or by one double decrease.

Wrap the yarn twice around the right needle, counter-clockwise. On the following row, it is usual to knit into the first loop, then purl the second.

Make one (m1 or M1)

This increase makes a small hole in the knitting and is used for shaping and for lace stitch patterns. When used for shaping, it is usually placed one or two stitches (or more) in from the edge of the knitting. The small holes made by the increases are easy to count.

1 ▍ At the required position, pick up the bar of yarn between the needles onto the right needle tip, inserting the right needle tip from front through to back.

2 ▍ Wrap the yarn around the right needle as if to knit and then pull the new stitch through beneath the bar, allowing the bar to drop from the right needle.

Make one through back loop (m1tbl or M1tbl): invisible increase

This useful increase is used to make a firm increase with no visible hole so it is sometimes called the invisible increase. The increased stitch sits neatly between two stitches so it must be worked at least one stitch in from the edge of the work. It is often used when forming darts (page 84).

1 ▍ At the required position, lift the bar between the needles with the left needle tip, inserting the needle from front through to back.

2 ▍ Insert the right-hand needle into the loop from right to left and wrap the yarn around counter-clockwise, as shown here.

3 ▍ Pull through, letting the loop fall off the needle in the usual way. Unlike other methods for making extra stitches, no hole is formed.

Decreasing

Decreasing is used to shape knitting, for example at an armhole or neckline. Decreases may also be used as part of textured or lace stitch patterns, when each decrease is usually balanced by a corresponding increase (see pages 54–55). Different methods of decreasing produce stitches that slope either to the right or the left.

115

Decrease methods

The basic decrease methods are knit two together; purl two together; slip, slip, knit; and purl two together through the back loops. In making these decreases, one of the two combined stitches is pulled over the other, creating a stitch that slopes to the left or right. This can be turned into an attractive feature, with balanced left- and right-sloping stitches on each side of a garment front, for example. You can also decrease by two stitches at once, if desired, or have a decrease that slopes neither to the left or the right—the vertical double decrease.

Knit two together (k2tog or K2tog)

This decrease slopes to the right, as you can see in the photographs here.

1 Insert the right needle through the first two stitches on the left needle, from left to right.

2 Wrap the yarn as usual and knit both stitches together.

Sip, slip, knit (ssk or Ssk)

This stitch slopes to the left and creates a mirror image of the K2tog decrease.

1 Slip the first stitch knitwise. Slip the second stitch knitwise. (They must be slipped one at a time).

2 Insert the left needle tip through the front loops of both slipped stitches together. Wrap the yarn around the right needle tip, as shown.

3 Lift the two slipped stitches over the yarn and off the needle, leaving one new stitch on the right needle.

Purl two together (p2tog or P2tog)

This decrease is worked on a wrong side row and makes a stitch that slopes to the right on the right side of the work.

Insert the right needle purlwise through the first and second stitches together. Wrap the yarn and purl both stitches together.

Set-in sleeve head

A set-in sleeve head is shaped in a curve.

Ssk at the end of right side rows and P2tog tbl at the beginning of wrong side rows decreases the edge sharply.

Remaining stitches bound off knitwise on a right side row.

Ssk at the end of right side rows creates stitches that slope to the left, against the edge.

K2tog at the beginning of right side rows and P2tog at the end of wrong side rows decreases the edge sharply.

K2tog at the beginning of right side rows creates stitches that slope to the right, against the edge.

Stitches bound off purlwise on a wrong side row.

Stitches bound off knitwise on a right side row.

⊚TRY IT

116 **Slipping stitches**

To slip a stitch is to pass it from one needle to the other without working into it. Various methods of decreasing (and many stitch patterns) require stitches to be slipped either knitwise or purlwise. The way you slip a stitch will affect the final appearance.

Slip one knitwise (sl1, Sl1, s1, or S1)

Slipping a stitch knitwise causes it to twist.

Insert the right needle into the stitch as if to knit it and slip it from the left needle onto the right.

Slip one purlwise (sl1p, Sl1p, s1p, or S1p)

When a stitch is slipped purlwise it remains untwisted.

Insert the right needle into the stitch as if to purl it and slip it from the left needle onto the right.

FIX IT

117 *Don't recognize a decrease method?*

Sometimes knitting instructions may specify other methods of decreasing. The abbreviation key should tell you how to work them. If the decreases form part of a lace or other stitch pattern, work them as instructed or the appearance of the pattern may be affected. If the decreases form part of the shaping, work a small swatch, decreasing as the instructions specify, then decide whether the decreases are intended to slope to the left or right and substitute the appropriate method. Common examples are "Slip 1, K1, pass the slip stitch over" and "K2tog through back loops. "Both methods form a stitch that slopes to the left, so you can substitute "slip, slip knit."

Purl two together through back loops (p2togtbl or P2togtbl)
This decrease is worked on a wrong side row and slopes to the left on the right side of the work.

1 With the yarn at the front of the work, insert the right needle through the back loop of the second stitch, then through the back loop of the first, from back through to front.

2 Wrap the yarn and purl both stitches together.

Raglan sleeve head
Shown here worked with "fully-fashioned" decreasing. This means that the decreases are all worked a few stitches in from the edge (one stitch in shown here), using methods to correspond with the slope of the shaping.

K2tog, K1 at the end of right side rows and P1, P2tog at the beginning of wrong side rows creates a sharp slope to the right.

K1, ssk at the beginning of right side rows and P2tog, P1 at the end of wrong side rows creates a sharp slope to the left.

K2tog, K1 at the end of right side rows creates a gentle slope to the right.

K1, ssk at the beginning of right side rows creates a gentle slope to the left.

Double decrease

Sometimes you need to decrease two stitches at the same time.

Knit three together (k3tog or K3tog): Work in a similar way to K2tog, knitting 3 stitches together. This creates a slope to the right on a right side row.

Purl three together (P3tog or p3tog or): Work in a similar way to P2tog, purling 3 stitches together. Worked on a wrong side row, creates a slope to the right on the right side of the work.

Knitwise double decrease: Slip one stitch knitwise, knit two together and then pass the slip stitch over. This creates a slope to the left on a right side row.

Purlwise double decrease: Purl two stitches together, slip the new stitch back to the left needle without twisting it then lift the next stitch on the left needle over the new stitch and off. Slip the decreased stitch purlwise onto to the right-hand needle. Worked on a wrong side row, this creates a slope to the left on the right side of the work.

Working vertical double decrease (s2togpo, S2togpo, dd, or DD)

This method decreases two stitches at the same time, creating a vertical stitch at the center. It is often used as a decorative feature, for example when shaping darts (page 84), or working chevron patterns (page 96).

1 ❙ Insert the right needle knitwise through the first and second stitches together.

2 ❙ Slip both stitches together onto the right needle. Knit the next stitch in the usual way.

3 ❙ Use the left needle to lift the two slipped stitches over the knitted stitch and off the right needle.

ADVANCED TECHNIQUES

From constructional details such as selvages, button bands, pockets, and darts through to the intricacies of lace knitting, edgings, and frills, the skills described in this chapter will enable you to produce knitting with a professional finish.

Selvages

Selvages are often worked at the side edges of a piece of knitting. They stabilize the edges, making it easier to join seams (page 140) or pick up stitches (page 62). A selvage may also be used to create a finished edge with no further added border. A selvage is formed at one or both side edges of a piece of knitting by working one or two edge stitches in a different way.

In this Rowan V-necked sweater, selvages around the arms are a subtle feature that adds texture and interest, as well as making it easier to set the sleeves into the armholes.

Selvage stitches

Garter-stitch selvage

This is the simplest selvage and is often used on stockinette stitch where side edges will be joined into seams, or where stitches will later be picked up. The selvage stitches are knitted on every row.
For a selvage at each side edge of the work:
First row: K1, work to the last stitch, K1.
Repeat this row.

Slip garter selvage

This selvage is firmer than the garter-stitch selvage and is therefore useful for stitch patterns that tend to spread widthwise, such as the garter-stitch ridge pattern shown here. Each selvage stitch is slipped (knitwise, page 57) on one row and knitted on the next row.
For a selvage at each side of the work:
First row: Slip 1, work to last stitch, K1.
Repeat this row.

Chain-stitch selvage

This selvage makes a neat edge for garter stitch (page 49). Each selvage stitch is slipped as described below on one row, and knitted on the next row.

For a selvage at each edge of the work:

First row: With the yarn in front (as if to purl), slip the first stitch knitwise (page 57), take the yarn to the back between the needle tips and knit to the end.

Repeat this row.

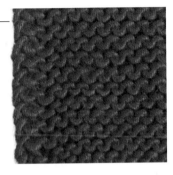

Slip-stitch selvage

Chain loops form along this selvage, one chain for every two rows of knitting. Use this selvage where stitches will later be picked up, to make a neat join that is less bulky than other methods.

For a selvage at each edge of the work:

Right side row: Slip 1 knitwise, work to the last stitch, K1.

Wrong side row: Slip 1 purlwise, work to the last stitch, P1.

Repeat these 2 rows.

Double garter-stitch selvage

This firm selvage is used for unattached edges that will require no further finishing, for example on a scarf.

For a selvage at each edge of the work:

First row: Slip 1 knitwise tbl, K1, work to the last 2 stitches, K2.

Repeat this row.

Picot selvage

This is a decorative selvage for unattached edges that will require no further finishing, for example on a shawl or baby blanket. (For details of how to work a yarn over (yo), see page 54.)

For a selvage at each edge of the work:

Right side row: Yo (taking yarn to back of right needle), K2tog, work to the last 2 stitches, ssk.

Wrong side row: Yo (wrapping yarn all around right needle, ending with yarn at front), P1, work to the last 2 stitches, P2.

Repeat these 2 rows.

⊚TRY IT

120 Make a wider border

Adapt the double garter-stitch selvage to make a wider border at one edge only, for example on a jacket front. For a border six stitches wide, work:

First row: Slip 1 knitwise tbl, K5, work to the end.

Second row: Work to the last 6 stitches, K6.

Repeat these 2 rows.

Picking up stitches

Sometimes you need to pick up stitches along one or more edges of a piece of knitting in order to continue the work in another direction—to construct sideways-knitted bands, or for a neckband or collar, for example. Stitches may be picked up from a side edge, a cast-on edge, or a bound-off edge.

Picking up stitches from a side edge

To space the required number of stitches evenly along an edge, divide the edge into a convenient number of equal sections with pins. Pick up the same number of stitches from each section, following the instructions given here.

Picking up on a curved edge

121

On a shaped edge, such as a neckline, you may obtain a neater finish by inserting the needle one-half of a stitch (one thread) in from a side edge, depending on the method used for the decreasing.

1 | With the right side of the work facing, insert the needle tip one whole stitch in from the edge. If the side edge is made with a selvage stitch (page 60), as here, it's easier to see where to insert the needle.

2 | Wrap the yarn around the tip in the usual way and draw the new loop through, making a new stitch on the needle. Repeat as required. On the side edge of stockinette stitch, picking up approximately three stitches for every four rows will result in a neat, flat join that is neither stretched nor puckered.

Picking up stitches from a bound-off edge

With the right side of the work facing, insert the needle tip through the center of each stitch of the last row, wrap the yarn and pull the new stitch through in the usual way. Picking up one stitch in each stitch of a bound-off edge makes a neat, firm line.

Picking up stitches from a cast-on edge

With the right side of the work facing, insert the needle tip in the space between two stitches of the first row, wrap the yarn, and pull through in the usual way.

The neckline of this sweater was finished by binding off at the back neck to give a firm shoulder line that will not stretch out of shape. Stitches at the center front here were left on a holder for a flat, seamless join. To work a collar like this, use a circular needle or set of double-pointed needles (page 10), and begin knitting up the collar stitches at the center front. Next, pick up the required stitches all around the remaining neck edge, ending by knitting up the remaining center-front stitches. Work in rows of the required stitch pattern, turning at the center front on each row. Bind off loosely in knit and purl as set, using a larger needle so the edge of the collar will lie flat.

122 **Using stitch holders**

For necklines, groups of stitches may be left on holders at the center front and back neck and then knitted up directly as part of a neckband or collar. Stitch holders may also be used when constructing pockets (page 76) or other details.

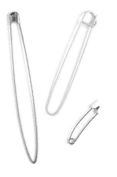

Stitch holders are like large safety pins, with blunt points. You can also use a double-pointed needle with a point protector on each end, or thread the stitches onto contrasting yarn with a tapestry needle and then tie the yarn ends together to keep the stitches from unraveling.

Placing stitches on a holder

Cut the yarn, leaving a long tail if this can be used later for assembly, or a 4in (10cm) tail to be run in after completion. Slip the stitches purlwise (page 48) onto the holder and close the holder.

Working stitches from a holder

It is usual to work stitches from a holder with the right side of the work facing. If the holder is fastened at right of the stitches, simply open the holder and work the stitches from it in the usual way. Otherwise, slip the stitches from the holder purlwise onto a small-size needle, then knit or purl them, as required, using the correct needle size.

FIX IT

123 *Picked up edge looks gappy and untidy?*

Sometimes picking up the required number of stitches along an edge leaves gaps between stitches. To correct this, pick up more stitches than required (e.g. 1 stitch from every row on the side edge of stockinette stitch) and then decrease evenly across the next row down to the correct number of stitches.

124 *Picked-up edge is too bulky?*

When working with bulky yarns, it may be better to insert the needle just one-half of a stitch in from a side edge to reduce bulk. This works best with textured yarns that will disguise any loose stitches.

125 *Neckline too loose?*

If stitches are left on holders at the center back and/or front of a neckline and then knitted up into a neckband, the neckline may be too loose and pull out of shape. Instead of leaving the stitches on holders, bind them off and pick them up again. The bound-off neckline will add structure to the shape.

126 *Neckline too tight?*

Leaving stitches on holders instead of binding them off will make a tight neckline looser and more flexible. If a bound-off edge of a neckband is too tight, unpick the binding-off and re-work it using a needle one or two sizes larger.

Ribs, hems, and other borders

The usual band of ribbing around the lower edge of a garment is called the welt. Similar bands of ribbing are often used for the cuffs of sleeves. Ribbing is a common choice for welts, cuffs, and collars because the unattached edge will not curl and it pulls in the width of the garment slightly, making a neat fit. However, there are other choices if elasticity is not required. Knitted hems make neat, flat edges, as do various stitch patterns such as garter stitch and seed stitch, for example.

127 Ribbing

As a rule, any ribbed border is worked on needles two sizes smaller than those used for the main parts of the garment. Use the cable cast-on method or the thumb cast-on method (page 45), to make an elastic edge.

Knit 1, purl 1 rib

The easiest rib to work is K1, P1 rib. Cast on an even number of stitches.
Row 1: * K1, P1, * repeat from * to * to end. Repeat this row.

Knit 2, purl 2 rib

K2, P2 rib is more elastic than K1, P1 rib. Cast on a multiple of 4 stitches plus 2.
Row 1: * K2, P2, * repeat from * to * to last 2 stitches, K2.
Row 2: * P2, K2, * repeat from * to * to last 2 stitches, P2.
Repeat these 2 rows.

128 Straight hem

A hem is formed by working stockinette stitch to twice the hem depth required and then folding the lower edge to the wrong side and securing it in place. A purl row, worked on the right side of the piece, makes a neat fold line so the hem will lie flat. Knitting-up the lower edge of the hem makes the neatest finish.

1 | Make a provisional cast-on edge by casting on with suitable waste yarn (such as a smooth cotton yarn), and knit 1 row. Change to the main yarn and needles one or two sizes smaller than used for main parts of garment. * Beginning with a P row, work an odd number of rows in stockinette stitch, ending with a P row.*
Fold-line row (right side row): P to end. Repeat from * to *.

2 | With the right side of the work facing, fold the cast-on edge up behind the needle so the loops of the first row in main color match the stitches on the needle. Pick up a larger needle (as used for main parts) and knit the first stitch from the left-hand needle together with the corresponding loop from the first row in main color. Repeat for each stitch along the row. Note that there will be one loop less than the number of stitches on the needle, so knit the last stitch on the needle by itself.

3 | Continue as required on larger needles. Remove the provisional cast-on. Press the hem carefully, and it will lie quite flat.

129 Picot hem

Give a straight hem a picot edge by replacing the purl row fold-line with a row of decreases and corresponding yarn overs. Work as for the straight hem over an odd number of stitches but work the following fold-line row (right side row):
* K2tog, yo, * repeat from * to * to last st, K1.

130 Gauge it

Carefully check the gauge for the border stitch on needles two sizes smaller than used for the main part, and figure out how many stitches are needed for the welt or cuff. You also need to know how many stitches you need for the main part on larger needles. Knit the welt or cuff and then on the first row of the main part (using larger needles) increase several stitches evenly spaced along the row to make the total number you need. The invisible increase (page 55) is usually the best method to use.

131 Garter stitch edging

A garter stitch edging will not curl, but it is not elastic and tends to spread widthwise. Use needles at least 2 sizes smaller than those used for the main parts of the garment.

Cast on any number of stitches.
Row 1: K to end. Repeat this row.
For the neatest result following a cable cast-on (page 44), count the first row as a wrong-side row and knit an odd number of rows.

For the neatest result following a thumb cast-on (page 45), count the first row as a right-side row and knit an even number of rows.

132 Single seed stitch edging

Like garter stitch, this stitch will not curl at the edges and is non-elastic. Use needles one or two sizes smaller than for the main part of the work.

Cast on an odd number of stitches using either the cable cast-on or thumb cast-on (see pages 44–45).
Row 1: *K1, P1, * repeat from * to * to last stitch, K1. Repeat this row.

The cuffs and welt of this sweater, designed by Martin Storey for Rowan, feature easy-to-knit textured bands that lift it out of the ordinary.

⊚TRY IT

133 Alternative stitches

Try some fancy rib stitches, incorporating twists, cables or other stitch effects—most of them will do the same job as ordinary ribbing.

Consider using chevron stitches, which will lie quite flat and form decorative, zigzag edges for knitting. (See pages 96 for more examples of chevron stitches.)

Adding bands and borders

A band or border may be added to the edge of any piece of knitting to prevent it from curling, such as on the front edges of a cardigan or jacket, or all around a baby blanket. Use a stitch that lies flat, such as ribbing, garter stitch or seed stitch, or construct a knitted hem or a rolled edge. Bands and borders are normally knitted on needles one or two sizes smaller than those used for the main parts and are normally about 1–2in (2.5–5cm) wide. To add buttonholes, see page 78.

134 Vertical-knit bands

Bands knitted vertically need to be at a tighter gauge than the main part. Rib bands must therefore be made separately and sewn into place.

Working add-on ribbing

Work the band on smaller needles than the main parts. Work to the length required without binding off—it should be slightly stretched when sewn into place—then sew on the band and adjust the length to fit; bind off. For a ladder stitch seam (page 140), add one selvage stitch at the edge of the main part. Use a flat seam (no selvage required) if preferred.

Working extended ribbing

1 | For a neater lower edge, add enough extra stitches to the width of the lower ribbing for the side ribbing and then leave them on a holder when you change to larger needles. Increase 1 stitch at the edge to be worked as a selvage stitch (page 60) and taken into the seam.

2 | Once you have completed the main part on larger needles, use smaller needles to complete the vertical band, adding a selvage stitch at the inner edge for a neat seam.

135 Begin with the buttonholes

When working a vertical band with buttonholes, always begin with the buttonhole end. Then you can adjust the final length to suit without having to re-position the buttonholes.

136 Joining on yarn

If you need to join in a new ball of yarn on a vertical-knit band, do this at the inner edge of the band where the tails may be run in along the seam.

FIX IT

137 *Vertical knit band too tight?*

If this type of band is too short, it will gather up the edge of the knitting. Unravel band seam, unravel the bound-off edge, and add a few more rows.

138 *Vertical knit band too loose?*

A band that is too long will form a wavy edge. Unpick the band seam and unravel a few rows to adjust the length.

139
Horizontal-knit bands

For these bands, stitches are picked up evenly along the edge of the main garment pieces.

Adding a rib band

The main part should be worked with one selvage stitch (page 60) along the edge. Pick up the required stitches (see page 62) on smaller needles; space them evenly and pick up the correct number or the band will be too tight or too loose (three stitches from every four rows is a good rule of thumb). This band may also be worked in other rib stitches, garter stitch, seed stitch, and so on.

Working a rolled edge

If a band is worked in stockinette stitch, it will roll to the outside, purl side out. (For the band to roll to the inside, work in reverse stockinette stitch). Change to a larger needle to bind off to prevent a tight edge.

Adding a knitted hem

For a band to match a knitted hem, instead of casting on, pick up the required stitches. Work as given for the knitted hem (page 64), or the knitted hem with picots (page 65), then bind off and sew the bound-off edge into place.

140
Integral bands

Stitches such as garter stitch and seed stitch normally knit to a tighter row tension than other stitches. A group of such stitches worked as a wide selvage on the main part will form a firm, flat edge.

Including a garter stitch band

Add a lower border and band in garter stitch, knitted at the same time and on the same needles as the stockinette stitch main part. Work the edge stitch as a garter selvage stitch (page 60) for a neat finish. To avoid mistakes, place a ring marker on the needle between the band stitches and the main part, and slip it on every row.

Including a seed stitch border

Add a border of seed stitches (page 65) at the same time as working the main parts. Here, the borders, bands, and collar of this jacket were knitted in seed stitch at the same time as the stockinette stitch.

141
Mitered corners

Sometimes you want a band to fit around a corner: decreasing at an inward corner or increasing at an outward corner makes a neat miter.

Making an inward miter

At an inward corner, such as a V-neck, decrease the stitches of a picked-up band at either side of the corner. It is important to pick up one stitch exactly in the corner, to act as the center of the miter. This V-neck has an odd number of stitches, so the center stitch (marked here with a safety pin) was left on a holder when shaping the neck, and knitted up later with the neckband stitches. This rib neckband is decreased with a double decrease (page 59), centered on the marked stitch, on every alternate row.

Making an outward miter

At an outward corner, such as on a blanket border, stitches must be increased to form the miter. Use a circular needle to pick up the stitches along the required edges, and mark the corner stitch with a split ring marker or safety pin. On this garter stitch border, one stitch is increased using the invisible increase (page 55) at either side of the marked corner stitch on every alternate row. The corner stitch itself is worked as a stockinette stitch to emphasize the detail.

Armholes and sleeve shapes

Whether you are following knitting instructions or inventing your own design, it helps to understand how different types of armholes and sleeve shapes are constructed. Here are the classic shapes you need to understand.

Garment measurements: to include ease as detailed for each armhole style (see page 24)

A Width of front (= width of back)

B Depth of armhole

C Body measurement from center back neck to wrist

D Sleeve length (measured vertically, not along the sloping edge). A full-length sleeve normally begins at the

wrist. A three-quarter-length sleeve begins between wrist and elbow, and a short sleeve begins between elbow and underarm, as indicated on the diagrams.

E Wrist

F Top edge of sleeve

142

Drop shoulder

Suitable for: casual and children's garments, including babywear.
Ease: generous fit; add extra depth to armhole.

Working the front and back

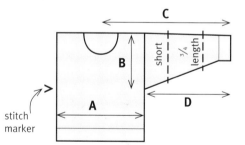

stitch marker

Working the sleeve

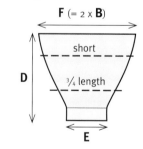

Designed by Sarah Hatton for Rowan, this comfortably yet elegant shrug cardigan features a textured stitch pattern that runs continuously along the three-quarter length sleeves and all the way across the back yoke.

For easy assembly, place stitch markers at each end of the first armhole row on both the front and back. Continue without any armhole shaping to the armhole depth required (B). The shoulders may be bound-off straight, or evenly sloped over four or six rows as for a set-in armhole (opposite).

The sleeve length D = C minus $\frac{1}{2}$ A. Note that D is often shorter than the actual (body) length of the arm due to the generous ease added to the body width. The width at the top of sleeve F = twice B. For a neat finish, subtract about $\frac{3}{8}$in (1cm) from F, and bind off loosely, so the top edge is slightly stretched when sewn in place.

143
Square armhole

Suitable for: casual and children's garments.
Ease: generous fit; add extra depth to armhole.

Working the front and back

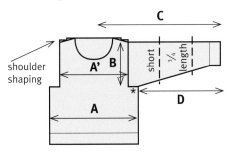

Working the sleeve

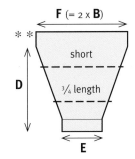

Shape the armhole at * by binding off 1–2in (2.5–5cm) at the beginning of two consecutive rows to reduce the width to A'. Continue without further armhole shaping to required depth (B). The shoulders may be bound-off straight, or evenly sloped over four or six rows as for a set-in armhole (below).

The width at the top of the sleeve F = twice B. Sleeve length D = C minus ½ A. Add extra rows (without shaping) at ** to match the stitches bound off at * on the front and back.

144
Set-in sleeve

Suitable for: neatly fitting and tailored garments for adults and children (easily layered under a coat or jacket).
Ease: close to medium fit.

Working the front and back

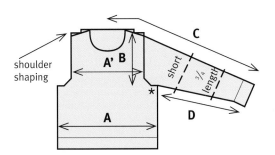

Working the sleeve

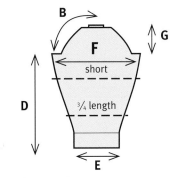

A neat set-in sleeve fits the armhole exactly.

At the armholes, bind off about 1in (2.5cm) of stitches at the beginning of two consecutive rows, at *. Then decrease on every alternate row to reach the required width across at the shoulder (A'). Continue without further armhole shaping to the required depth (B). The shoulders are normally shaped by dividing the remaining stitches into two or three groups, then binding off the groups over the next four or six rows.

The underarm sleeve length D should match the body measurement. To find the depth of the sleeve head G, add ½ of A' to D, then subtract the total from C. To shape the sleeve head, begin by binding off two groups of stitches to match those bound-off on the body. Curved measurement B on the sleeve should match B on the Front and Back. To form the curve, decrease on every alternate row, then on every row toward the top, then bind off the top edge at about 4 inches (10cm) wide.

145

Raglan sleeve

Suitable for: casual or relaxed-fit garments for all the family, including babies.
Ease: medium to generous fit.

Working the front and back

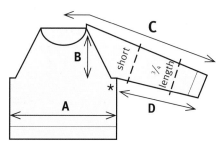

At the armholes at *, bind off about 1in (2.5cm) of stitches at the beginning of two consecutive rows. Decreasing at the armhole edges on every alternate row will often give the correct slope. On reaching depth B, the remaining width should equal that required for the back neck.

Working the sleeve

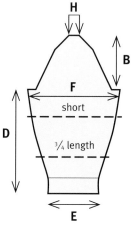

The sleeve dimensions can be calculated as follows: The underarm sleeve length D should match the body measurement. The raglan depth B should exactly match B on the front and back, with the same number of rows. The few stitches remaining at the top edge of the sleeve (H) will form part of the neck edge. To shape the raglan, begin by binding off two groups of stitches to match those bound-off on the body. Decrease on every alternate row and then on every row to complete the depth B to match the body. Grouping the every-row decreases toward the top of the sleeve prevents tightness across the shoulders.

Designed by Martin Storey for Rowan, the raglan sleeves and cozy front pockets make this a relaxed, informal sweater for everyday wear. The garter-stitch "V" at the neckline is a lovely textural detail.

FIX IT

146 *Sleeves too long?*

Take out a few rows above the cuff as follows: pull out a row the required distance above the cuff, picking up the loops of the row above on a needle (page 62). Decrease the stitches on the first row as necessary and re-knit the cuff downward from this point.

147 *Sleeves too short?*

Unravel down to the beginning of the sleeve-head shaping, and add extra rows as required. Or, pull out the row just above the cuff and re-knit a longer cuff downward from this point.

Made in a lightweight yarn, this women's mini batwing jumper with striped sleeves is both easy to knit and comfortable to wear—perfect for dressing up for the evening or down for casual wear.

Batwing

Suitable for: casual, relaxed, fun and party wear. May not layer under a coat or jacket; suits lightweight yarns and open stitches.
Ease: generous or very generous fit.

Working all in one

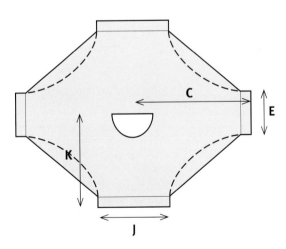

A batwing sweater may be knitted in one main piece, beginning at the lower edge (J) and increasing to the maximum width (twice C, less any cuffs). Shape the neck to finish at the required length K, work straight to complete the cuff length E, and then decrease the back to match the front. Stitches for cuffs may then be picked up and worked downward. Alternatively, the batwing shape may be worked sideways, from cuff to cuff. For a less bulky batwing, the shape may follow the dashed outlines.

⊚TRY IT

149 Test the fit

Knit the front(s) and back of the garment, and one sleeve. Assemble the pieces and try them on before working the second sleeve.

150 Knit from the top down

Sleeves for the drop-shoulder and square armhole shapes may be knitted from the top downward: join the shoulder seams, then pick up (page 62) the correct number of stitches from the side edges of the armhole rows and work down to the wrist.

151 Plot the shapes

For set-in and raglan shapes try plotting the shapes on graph paper as explained on page 39.

152 Knitting flair

A sleeve knitted the same width from wrist to underarm will appear slightly flared when worn; for a wider flare (dashed outline), begin with more stitches at the lower edge and decrease to the underarm. Combine this with any type of sleeve head: a flared set-in sleeve is shown here.

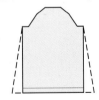

153 All puffed up

A puffed sleeve may be fitted into a set-in armhole: shape the sleeve head less sharply, so that measurement B is 1–2in (2.5–5cm) longer than B on the body, and the top edge is wider. Gather the top edge of the sleeve to fit the armhole.

Necklines, neckbands, and collars

The neckline of a sweater or jacket may be shaped in several ways, and finished with a band or collar. The basic shapes are shown here. The proportions and details can be varied in many different ways.

156 Round neckline on a sweater

At the back neck edge (A), stitches may be bound off or left on a holder and knitted up later to construct the neckband or collar. To shape the front neck edge at depth B, stitches are normally divided into approximate thirds. The center group is bound off or left on a holder, and the groups at each side are decreased to shape the neckline, as shown here. Some possible finishes are given below.

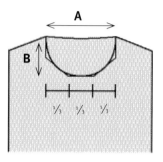

⊚TRY IT

154 Try other stitch patterns

Bands and collars don't have to be in ribbing: other stitches such as garter stitch and seed stitch are also suitable. Make sure the finished opening on a sweater is large enough for the head because these stitches are less elastic than ribbing.

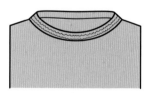

155 Work both sides at once

Here the two sides of the front neck shaping are being worked at the same time, using two separate balls of yarn. This makes it easy to match the shaping so both sides are exactly the same.

Working a crew neckband

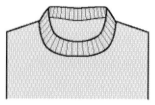

Pick up stitches (page 62) all around the neck opening and work them for the depth required. A double neckband may be worked to twice the depth required and then folded in half to the inside (or outside) and sewn into place.

Adding a small roll collar

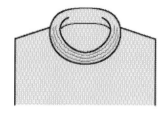

Pick up stitches in the same way as for a crew neckband, but work them in stockinette stitch, with the purl side inside—using circular needles (page 102) avoids a seam. When bound off loosely, the knitting rolls with the purl side outside.

Creating a funnel neck

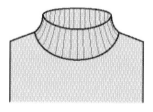

Make the neck opening rather wide and shallow; the neckband stitches may be decreased at either side for a neat fit.

Adding a large roll neck

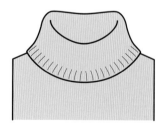

Make the neck opening rather wide and shallow. Pick up stitches as for a crew neckband and work to the depth required.

Making a simple collar

Pick up stitches for a collar on circular needles (page 102) and work in rows beginning and ending at the center front. Or, a collar may be knitted separately and sewn in place.

Adding a collar stand

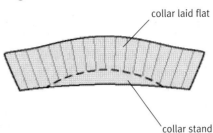

collar laid flat

collar stand

A collar often needs extra depth at the back neck so that it will sit flat. Extra rows of short-row shaping may be included to form a collar stand (page 86–87).

157

Round neckline on a jacket

When a garment is open at the front—a cardigan, jacket, or vest—the top edges of the front bands form part of the neck edge. Below are some possible finishes, ranging from a neckband to a collar.

FIX IT

158 *Collar won't sit flat, even with a collar stand?*

Make sure the outer edge is not too tight by using a needle one or two sizes larger for the bind-off row.

159 *Neck opening too small to fit over head?*

This is a common problem with children's sweaters. If the neckband has a seam at one shoulder, unpick the neckband seam and one shoulder seam. Add a crochet edge (page 138) with one or two button loops. Sew on the buttons. If the neckband is circular knit, unravel it and unpick one shoulder seam. Re-knit the neckband in rows and then add the crochet edge.

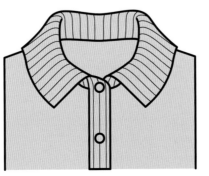

button

button loop

single crochet

160 *Want a lower neckline at the back?*

Shape the back neckline in a similar way to the front neckline, over the last few rows.

Fitting a jacket crew neckband

For a neat fit, place the top button on the neckband, perhaps with another button just below, at the top of the front bands, to avoid gaping. The front bands shown are picked up and worked in ribbing along the front edges (page 67), with the neckband added last.

Adding a jacket collar

The side edges of this collar begin and end halfway across the top edges of the front bands, so that they meet at the center without overlapping.

Working a polo shirt collar

Work the front bands lengthwise and sew in place; the collar continues upward, forming an overlap at the center front.

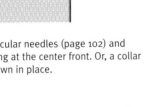

V-neck on a sweater

When making the body, the back neck edge (A) stitches may be bound off, or left on a holder and used to construct the neckband or collar. To shape the front neck edge, stitches are decreased at each side, evenly spaced over the depth B, which may be shallow or deep, as indicated. There are several V-neck finishes suitable for a sweater, dress, or other non-opening garment, as described below.

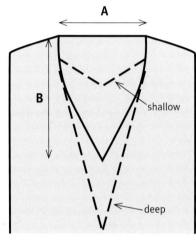

Adding a ribbed V-neck edging

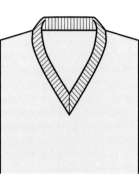

Pick up stitches (page 62) around the neck edge on circular needles (page 102) and decrease sharply at the center front to make a neat miter (page 67).

Making an overlapping neckband

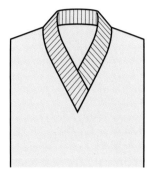

If the neckband is worked in rows, beginning and ending at center front, without any decreasing, the ends may be overlapped and sewn down as shown here.

Adding a collar to a V-neck

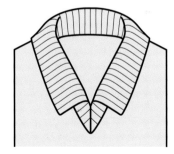

If desired, you can extend a rib v-neck into a collar, with or without a collar stand.

Making a shawl collar

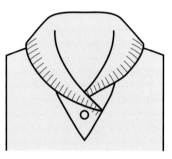

Extend an overlap neckband to form a shawl collar, like the one shown here (the button is optional).

Adding a collar stand

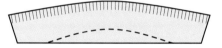

To increase the depth of a collar at the back neck for a smooth fit, make a collar stand with short row shaping (pages 86–87).

This simple collar on a round neckline is worked in double seed stitch.

162

V-neck on a jacket

A V-neck for a jacket or other front-opening garment is simple to make. The two fronts are worked separately, with matching decreasing. You may then wish to add one of the following finishes.

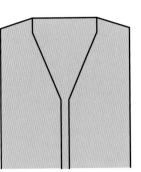

Making a lengthwise continuous band

Make the front band all in one piece, and sew in place up one front edge, around the back neck and down the other front edge. The top buttonhole should fall just level with the beginning of the front neck shaping.

Adding a collar

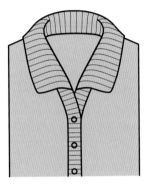

The front bands shown here have been picked up all around the front and neck edges—try a long-length circular needle—and extended into a collar around the neck.

Adding a collar stand

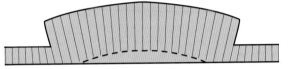

Add a collar stand to the neck edge to improve the fit (pages 86–87).

Adding a shawl collar

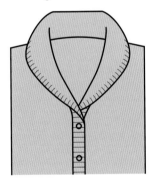

A shawl collar wraps warmly around the neck and is straightforward to work.

Adding a shawl collar with stand

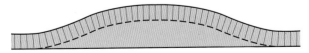

First work a large collar stand and then pick up stitches along both front edges to form the front bands and the collar edging (pages 86–87).

Designed by Jennie Atkinson for Rowan and knitted in a soft baby alpaca and merino yarn, the shirt-style collar and three-quarter length sleeves make this a classic, timeless garment.

Pockets

Keep bulk to a minimum by adding pockets to garments by one of these methods. To prevent unsightly bulges, pocket linings should be neatly stitched to straight rows and vertical lines of stitches, as described below.

163
Knitting a patch pocket

This pocket is applied to the right side of the garment and stitched in place.

1 | For a neat lower edge, pick up the required stitches from the main piece of knitting. Begin by slipping a small-size double-pointed needle through a straight line of stitches, picking up the left "leg" of each stitch, in the position required.

2 | Join in the yarn at the right of the stitches (leave a long tail for assembly) and use a correct-size needle to knit the stitches from the small-size needle.

3 | Knit the pocket to the required length, ending with a few rows of ribbing or other edging, as required, and bind off, leaving another long tail.

4 | Each side edge of the pocket should be sewn to a straight line of stitches. To make this easier, slip the small-size double-pointed needle through every alternate stitch along the required line. At the right pocket edge, thread a tapestry needle with the long yarn tail and take up one loop from the small-size needle, then one loop from the edge of the pocket; repeat to the top, matching the rows, and fasten off.

5 | Attach the left edge of the pocket in a similar way, but working from top to bottom, using the yarn tail left after binding off the pocket.

⊚TRY IT

164 Button up

Add a button to fasten a pocket. To do this, work a buttonhole near the top of a patch pocket, or just below a straight slit for a pocket, and sew on a button to match. On a diagonal slit, you could work a button loop halfway up the edge of the slit.

165
Knitting a diagonal-slit pocket

A diagonal-slit pocket has a shaped edge like a jeans pocket, and the only part visible on the front of the garment is the slit, which can be finished in a decorative stitch, if desired.

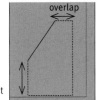

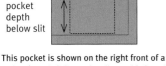

This pocket is shown on the right front of a jacket (on a left front, the slit would slope in the opposite direction).

1 **|** First, knit the pocket lining to the depth required below the lowest point of the diagonal slit, ending with a wrong side row. Leave the stitches on a spare needle or transfer to a stitch holder.

2 **|** Work to where the pocket slit is required to begin. Work the stitches to the right of the pocket slit and leave the remaining stitches to the left on a holder or a spare needle. Then work the whole area to the right of the pocket slit, decreasing as required for the diagonal slope up to the top of the pocket slit. Leave the remaining stitches on another holder or spare needle.

3 **|** With the right sides of both pieces facing, rejoin the yarn at the right of the pocket lining stitches and work across them, then work across the stitches from the holder at the left of pocket slit. Work without shaping on these stitches until the length exactly matches the length of the area to the right of the pocket slit, ending on a wrong side row. Break the yarn leaving a long tail.

4 **|** The number of stitches cast on for the pocket lining at step 1, less the number of decreases made for the diagonal slope, equals the number of stitches that overlap on the next row. With right side facing, work from the stitches on the second holder at step 2 until the overlap number remains. Then place the stitches left at the end of step 3 behind them, and work two stitches together (one from each needle) to the end of the overlap. Complete the row, and complete the front of the garment.

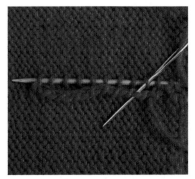

5 **|** Sew down the free edge(s) of the pocket lining in the same way as for a patch pocket (opposite), but on the wrong side of the work.

6 **|** The finished pocket blends neatly into the front of the garment. This diagonal slit pocket has been finished with a narrow garter stitch edging (page 65). For a matching diagonal slit pocket on the left front of a garment, work the stitches to the right of the slit along with the stitches from the pocket lining. Then work the stitches to the left of the slit, decreasing for the diagonal slope.

166
Working a straight slit pocket

Knit the pocket lining first. At the required position for the slit, on a right side row, bind off the same number of stitches as the pocket lining. On the following row, work to the bound-off stitches, then with wrong side of the pocket lining facing, work across the stitches from the pocket lining and complete the row. Sew down the free edges of the pocket lining as described in step 5 above. Depending on the stitch pattern, an edging may be required.

This straight pocket is hidden behind a deep welt of double seed stitch.

Making buttonholes

There are several ways to make buttonholes. Choose a method according to the type of garment: a heavy-weight jacket requires large buttons and strong buttonholes to resist stretching and fraying, whereas a baby garment needs small, flat buttons and the buttonholes will not be in use for more than a few months.

167
Working a two-row horizontal buttonhole

This buttonhole is worked by simply binding off on one row and then casting on again on the next row. The version given here provides the neatest result, with no gaps at the corners of the slit. Shown here is a 4-stitch buttonhole, worked on a 1 x 1 rib band, picked up from the front edge of a garment.

1 **I** Work to the position required for the buttonhole. Bind off 1 stitch less than the number required for the buttonhole (e.g., for a 4-stitch buttonhole, bind off next 3 stitches). Slip the last stitch from the right-hand needle to the left-hand needle (purlwise) and work it together with the next stitch. Complete the row.

2 **I** On the next row, work to the bound-off stitches. Turn the work and use the cable cast-on method (page 44) to cast on 1 stitch more than required for the buttonhole (e.g., for a 4-stitch buttonhole, cast on 5 stitches). Turn the work again and continue to the end of the row.

3 **I** On the following row, work to one stitch before the cast-on stitches. Work the next two stitches together and complete the row. You now have the original number of stitches.

4 **I** Continue to work rows as required in the pattern. The finished buttonhole has no loose stitches at the corners.

168
Sizing your buttonholes

Buy the buttons before working the buttonholes so you can size the holes for an exact fit. If a buttonhole is too loose, it will tend to come undone. If it is too tight, it will tend to fray in use. To determine the size of buttonhole required, place a button on a gauge sample (or appropriate area of the garment) of the stitch to be used for the bands, and count the width in stitches (for vertical buttonholes count the rows).

Work a trial band and buttonhole on the gauge sample—raised, rounded buttons need slightly larger buttonholes than flat buttons of the same diameter.

169
Spacing the buttonholes

On a jacket or cardigan, plan enough buttons and buttonholes for the band not to gap when worn. Work the button band first. Mark positions for the top and bottom buttons, about ½in (1.5cm) from each end of the band. Measure between these points and place more markers at equal intervals. Now work the buttonhole band to match, with a buttonhole to match each marker.

170

Working a one-row horizontal buttonhole

This buttonhole gives the neatest result of all and is ideal for chunky yarns and narrow bands that are only a few rows wide. It is shown here worked four stitches wide, on a garter stitch band.

1 | Work to the position required for the buttonhole. Slip the next stitch purlwise. With the yarn at back of the work, * Sl1p, pass the previous stitch over this stitch*, repeat from * to *, until the required number of stitches have been fastened off, i.e. 3 more times for a four-stitch buttonhole. Slip the last stitch purlwise back onto the left-hand needle.

2 | Turn the work around and use the cable cast-on method (page 44) to cast on one more stitch than required for the buttonhole, e.g. cast on 5 stitches for a 4-stitch buttonhole.

3 | Turn the work around again so the cast-on stitches are on the right-hand needle. Slip the next stitch purlwise (page 57) and pass the last cast-on stitch over it to close the gap. Complete the row.

4 | Continue to work rows as required in the pattern. The finished buttonhole has no holes at the corners.

171

Working a vertical buttonhole

Knitted in simple stockinette stitch, this cropped cardigan, which was designed for Rowan by Sarah Hatton, features bold buttons on a wide, ribbed button band.

This buttonhole is not as strong as the horizontal types but it is useful on narrow vertical-knit bands and for decorative purposes. A 6-row buttonhole is shown here on a seed-stitch band.

1 | Work to the position required for the slit, ending at the middle of a right-side row. Turn the work and work an even number of rows on the first set of stitches, so ending at the slit edge.

2 | Do not cut the yarn but join in another small ball and work the same even number of rows on the second set of stitches, so ending again at the slit edge. Cut the second ball, leaving a 6in (15cm) tail. Use the first ball of yarn to complete the row and continue the work.

3 | When the knitting is complete, use the starting and ending tails of the second ball to backstitch across the top and bottom of the slit, making it firmer, before running in the tails on the wrong side. Seed stitch makes neat, firm edges to the slit. In other stitches the edges may tend to curl.

Beautiful buttons

The button(s) you choose can make or mar your latest creation. Choose a size to suit your project: for baby garments, buttons should be small and flat; for a classic cardigan, choose a small to medium size that is not too heavy for the design; for chunky, casual jackets, large buttons are usually appropriate.

172

Choosing the right buttons

• For multi-colored or heavily textured knits, plain buttons in a toning color are usually the best choice; for plainer knits, you might prefer fancier buttons or a contrasting color to add extra interest.
• Buy the buttons before knitting the garment piece with the buttonholes so the latter can be made to fit. Take the gauge sample with you to help choose the button color. Otherwise, you should take the completed knitting with you and choose buttons to fit the buttonholes.
• For garments with several buttons, buy an extra one and sew it inside a side seam as a spare.

Wood, leather, glass, and pearl

Buttons made of natural materials add a special touch to knitwear in natural fibers. Choose wood, horn, or leather for rugged casual knits. For lighter, more feminine garments, choose delicate mother of pearl or glass. (Transparent buttons can be useful if you can't find a color match.)

Flat, two- and four-hole buttons

These are suitable for most purposes. For baby garments, choose a small size with minimum bulk to avoid discomfort. These buttons are normally sewn to knitwear with a thread shank, as at right.

Vintage buttons

Vintage buttons can be fascinating to collect. Search your collection for a quirky finishing touch to a purse or other accessory—you may even find yourself knitting a new project just to be able to use a special button.

Shanked buttons

Shanked buttons have no holes through the center; they are attached by sewing through the hole in the shank on the back. Because of the shank, they sit neatly when fastened through a buttonhole and are suitable for medium- to heavy-weight knits.

173

Marking the button positions

Buttons should be accurately spaced to match the position of the buttonholes.

Lay the garment flat with the buttonhole band overlapping the button band. Mark the position of each button on the button band by inserting a pin at right angles to the edge. To check the accuracy, count the rows (or stitches) between the pins; they should fall at regular intervals to match the buttonholes.

Novelty buttons

Novelty buttons should be used with caution on knitwear because any little projections or sharp corners (as on the teddy button, bottom right) will tend to catch on the buttonholes and fray them. Look for smooth, rounded shapes like the selection on the left-hand side.

174 Attaching a flat button

You can use knitting yarn and a yarn needle if the threaded needle will fit through the holes in the button. Otherwise, use sewing thread and any needle of a suitable size. For extra strength, use pearl cotton No. 5. Match the thread color to the knitting yarn or choose another color if you wish.

1 | Cut about 36in (90cm) of yarn or thread and thread the needle. Tie the two ends with an overhand knot. On the right side of the work, pass the needle beneath one stitch (two strands) of knitting, then through the loop above the knot. Pull the yarn through. Thread the button onto the needle.

2 | Hold the button flat at the correct position. Two-hole buttons should be placed so the holes are aligned with the buttonhole slit. Take the needle up and down through the holes several times, ending at the wrong side. Four-hole buttons may be stitched in several ways, as shown right, and centered at the buttonhole position.

3 | Bring the needle through to the right side beneath the button. Wind the thread tightly around the sewn stitches five or six times to make a little stalk (a shank). Take the needle through to the wrong side and fasten off with two small backstitches through the previous stitches.

175 Attaching a shanked button

Use a fairly strong thread such as pearl cotton No. 5 or linen thread because the hard shank can wear away yarn or weak thread.

Secure the thread as for a flat button and stitch several times through the hole in the shank. Fasten off on the wrong side as for a flat button.

176 Attaching buttons decoratively

Here are some ideas for attaching buttons decoratively to give a knitted garment added pizzazz. You may be able to come up with a few additional ideas.

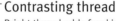

Contrasting thread
Bright thread adds focal interest to a plain button. Here a vintage two-hole coat button was attached with bright pink pearl cotton.

Stacked buttons
Two buttons of different sizes can be stacked together. Here, the pale blue button sits neatly in the central depression of the larger navy button. (Both buttons have two holes).

Bead detailing
This two-hole button was sewn on with a contrasting bead, using thread to match the bead.

Crossed threads
Try working the stitching in a cross formation on a four-hole button.

Square stitch
On a four-hole button try working the stitches between the holes to form a square.

Bird's-foot formation
A four-hole button can also be stitched in a bird's-foot formation, as shown here.

Parallel bars
Four-hole buttons can look smart sewn with two parallel bars of stitches. (This wooden button has been dyed pink).

Multiple beads
This four-hole button was attached using a square formation, with a bead added to each side of the square.

Fastenings

Knitted items may be closed with zippers or a range of drawstrings and ties. Zippers may be used to close garments, purses, or pillows. When correctly attached, they provide a neat fastening with no bulky layers. Use ties and drawstrings for garments and purses.

177 Choosing a zipper

Zipper weight Choose the weight of zipper to suit the knitting. Lightweight, dressmaking zippers will suit lightweight knits. For bulky knits you may prefer a heavy-weight zipper, or you can make a feature of a brass jeans zipper (short lengths only).

Length Zippers range from about 6in (15cm) to about 30in (76cm), although you can get other specialist sizes. The zipper should never be longer than the knitted edge or it will stretch the knitting out of shape. It is better to choose a slightly shorter zipper and leave a few rows of knitting unattached at the end than to choose a zipper that is too long. It is better still to purchase the zipper and then make the opening in the knitting to the exact length required.

Color Choose a color to tone with the knitting. If in doubt, a darker shade will usually look better than a lighter shade.

⊚ TRY IT

179 Decorate your zipper pull

You can purchase special decorative zipper pulls or make your own with beads, as on the pull shown in step 4 (below). Avoid decorating a zipper with pompons, tassels, or anything that is likely to catch in the teeth.

178 Attaching a zipper

Zippers should be sewn in place by hand. The vest front shown below is finished with a garter-stitch border, although a border is not necessary—a zipper can be placed directly between any two knitted edges. The two-stitch garter selvage (page 61) or a single crochet edge (page 139) will give a neat finish for a zipper.

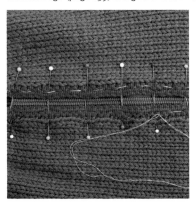

1 | With the right side of the knitting facing you, place one edge of the knitting just touching the zipper teeth. Knitting should not be stretched. Pin in place with pins at right angles to the edge. Use a sharp sewing needle and contrasting sewing thread to baste the zipper in place. Baste the top end of the zipper out of the way (see step 4). Pin and baste the other knitted edge in the same way. (Make sure any patterning or stripes match up exactly).

2 | With the wrong side facing you, whip stitch the outer edge of the zipper to the wrong side of the knitting. Pink thread was used here for clarity, but you should use thread to match the knitting yarn.

3 | With the right side facing you, backstitch close to the knitted edge: this garter-stitch border is backstitched just below the bind-off; on a side edge, backstitch one-half of a stitch in from the edge. Remove the basting.

4 | On this V-neck, the fabric tags at the top of the zipper are tucked slightly sideways, beneath the knitted edge. On a round neck garment, you may prefer to fold the tags back at a right angle.

180 Ties and drawstrings

Garments can also be fastened with one or more pairs of ties, made from I-cords (page 135), twisted cords (page 135), braids (page 135), crochet, or purchased ribbons or cords. Drawstrings are usually threaded through rows of eyelets (page 88). They may be used to secure a purse or to shape the waistline or the neckline of a garment.

A twisted cord tied in a neat bow provides a fun finishing touch on this cable-knit tea cozy.

Shoulder pads

Shoulder pads may be added to a sweater or jacket (usually with set-in sleeves) to emphasize the shoulder line. Ready-made shoulder pads are available in different sizes and thicknesses but knitted pads work well for knitwear because they can be made in matching yarn, so the color will never show through the garment. Also, they can be made with a slightly cupped shape, giving a smooth fit beneath knitwear.

Special abbreviations

Ktw = knit twice into the same stitch (page 54).
s2togpo = slip 2 stitches together, knit one then lift the 2 slipped stitches over the knitted one—vertical double decrease (page 59).

181 Knitting a shoulder pad

For bulky yarns, use the same yarn and needles as for the garment. Finer yarns may be doubled (or trebled).

1 | Cast on 3 stitches.
Inc. row: Ktw, knit to end.
Repeat this row until you have enough stitches to make a width of about 5in (12.5cm), ending with an odd number of stitches. Place a split ring marker on the central stitch.
Shaping row: Ktw, knit to 1 stitch before marker, S2togpo, knit to end.
Repeat inc row, 3 more times.
Repeat last 4 rows once or twice more, ending with enough stitches to make a width of 6–7in (15–17.5cm), and an odd number of stitches.
Bind off.

2 | Turn the garment wrong side out. Only the three corners of the pad are sewn in place: with the shoulder seam at the center, sew the two corners of the bound-off edge to the armhole seams. Sew the cast-on point to the shoulder seam, where it naturally falls, without stretching the seam or the pad.

⊚TRY IT

182 **Make a thicker shoulder pad**

Make two pieces and sew them back-to-back, adding a layer of batting between them for even more bulk.

Shaping with vertical darts

By decreasing (or increasing) within the body of the knitting instead of at the edges, the total width is reduced (or increased) in a similar way to sewing a dart in fabric. Vertical darts may be used to shape the top of a hat (page 109), to shape the yoke of a circular-knit sweater (page 108), or to shape the waist area of a tailored garment below the bust.

Special abbreviations

K1 = knit 1 (page 47).
K2tog = knit 2 together (page 56).
m1tbl = make one through back loop (page 55).
P1 = purl 1 (page 48).
s2togpo = vertical double decrease (page 59).
ssk = slip, slip, knit (page 56).
Tw2R = twist 2 to the right (see TwR, page 91).

183

Working darts

A dart is created by working a number of paired decreases (page 56) above each other, several rows apart. The number of decreases and the number of rows between them will vary according to the shape and size of dart required. Paired decreases may be worked at either side of a central stitch or next to each other, or double decreases (page 59) may be worked instead.

When working darts, slip a split-ring marker onto the knitting to mark the central stitch of each dart required.

Working a decreasing dart

Dec row (right side row): Work to 2 stitches before the marked stitch, ssk, work the central stitch, K2tog, work to the end (or to the next dart).
Work an odd number of rows (3 rows are shown here) without shaping, ending with a wrong-side row. Move the marker up every few rows.
Repeat these (4) rows as required.

Working a dart with double decreases

Dec row (right side row): Work to 1 stitch before the marked stitch, S2togpo, work to the end (or to the next dart).
Work an odd number of rows ending with a wrong side row.
Repeat these rows.
To increase after this dart, work the increasing dart as described left.

Decorative darts

Paired shapings for darts may be worked at either side of a small group of stitches, such as a cable, or the little twist in this example. There are 4 stitches between the paired shapings here, worked as "P1, Tw2R, P1" on right-side rows, and "K1, P2, K1" on wrong-side rows. The decreases and increases are worked in the same way as for the blue sample, left.

Working an increasing dart

Inc row (right side row): Work to the marked stitch, m1tbl, work the central stitch, m1tbl, work to the end (or to the next dart).
Work an odd number of rows.
Repeat these rows.

⊚ TRY IT

184 Try different increases/decreases

Other methods for decreasing and increasing may be used instead of ssk, K2tog, and m1tbl, giving a variety of decorative effects.

Positioning darts

To shape the waist of a garment (diagram 1) divide the number of stitches for the whole front by four. Normally, two darts are worked, each one-quarter of the width in from the side seams, as shown on the vest below. Place darts in corresponding positions on the back.

Determine the number of stitches to be decreased between hip and waist, and the number of rows over which the decreasing will take place. The fit should not be too tight or the knitting will stretch, and any front fastenings will gape.

Think of the dart as a section removed from the knitting. For example, suppose 24 stitches are to be decreased in total over 4 darts (2 front and 2 back), and the depth required is 24 rows. Each of 4 darts will decrease 6 stitches = 3 pairs of decreases. So over 24 rows, decreases may be worked on the 1st, 9th, and 17th rows (i.e. every 8 rows).

To shape a circular-knit sweater yoke (diagram 2) the total number of yoke stitches must divide exactly into a number of equal sections (e.g. 8, 10, or 12). Determine the number of stitches to be decreased between the bottom of the yoke and the neck opening.

For example, if there are 192 stitches at the bottom of the yoke, and the neck opening requires 80 stitches, then 112 stitches must be decreased. So the yoke may be divided into 8 equal sections, each of 24 stitches, decreasing down to 10 stitches at the neck edge. Each section will decrease by 14 stitches, i.e. 7 pairs of decreases.

Determine the depth of yoke in rounds, for example 48 rounds. For a neat fit at the neck, place the decreases closer together toward the top: for example, on the 1st and every following 6th round, 7 times in all, then on the following 4th round, twice (1st, 7th, 13th, 19th, 25th, 31st, 37th, 41st, and 45th rounds).

When shaping the top of a hat (diagram 3) the shapings are calculated in a similar way to a sweater yoke. Each section decreases down to just 1 or 2 stitches at the center top, where the remaining stitches are gathered tightly and secured. Again, the decreasing rows may be closer together toward the top of a rounded shape.

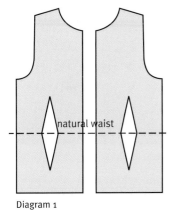

Diagram 1

Diagram 2

Yoke in 8 sections

Diagram 3

This hat is shaped with six darts, each decreasing down to two stitches at the top. The remaining twelve stitches are then gathered tightly and secured.

This vest is shaped with four waist darts, worked with paired decreases and a central stitch. In this case, each central stitch is worked in reverse stockinette to emphasize the vertical lines.

⊚ TRY IT

186 **Make a mock-up**

A quick way to determine the correct position and size of waist darts is to cut a front to size from a knitted fabric (such as cotton jersey), cut a slit for each dart, and pin the fabric to fit the waist. Then measure the fabric to calculate the equivalent knitted stitches.

Short-row shaping

By working only one section of a row and then turning the piece and working back again, one section of the knitting is made longer than the rest. The technique is sometimes called "partial knitting." It's great for adding unobtrusive curves or soft angles to otherwise straight areas—use it on socks, hats, or collar stands, or to shape garments for a true fit.

187

Working short-row shaping

To avoid making a hole where each row is turned, the adjacent stitch is "wrapped" as shown below. Wrapping may be worked knitwise or purlwise to match the stitch pattern in use. When a wrapped stitch is worked into as shown at right, the "step" formed by the short row is disguised, and the knitting appears perfectly even.

Working into wrapped stitches

When the short-row shaping is complete, the wrapped stitches are disguised on the next row as explained here.

Wrapping stitches

This example shows a collar stand in stockinette stitch. The short rows are worked at the center of the piece and may be represented diagrammatically as shown opposite.

1 ▌ Work the number of stitches required for the first short row. On this knit row the next stitch will be wrapped knitwise. Note that the wrapped stitch is not the last stitch of the short row but the next (unworked) stitch. With yarn at back of the work, slip the next stitch purlwise. Bring the yarn between the needle tips to the front of the work, as shown here.

2 ▌ Slip the stitch from the right needle back onto the left needle. Take the yarn to the back between the needle tips. One stitch has been wrapped knitwise.

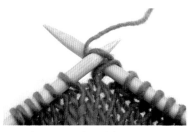

To work a wrapped stitch knitwise, insert the right needle under the wrap and then into the stitch (knitwise). Knit both the wrap and the stitch together.

3 ▌ Turn the work. The yarn is now at the front of the work, ready to purl the second short row. Purl the number of stitches required for the second short row. The next stitch will be wrapped purlwise. With the yarn at the front of the work, slip the next stitch purlwise. Take the yarn to the back of the work between the needle tips, as shown.

4 ▌ Slip the stitch from the right needle back onto the left needle. Bring the yarn to the front between the needle tips. One stitch has been wrapped purlwise. Turn the work. The yarn is now at the back of the work, ready to knit the third short row. Continue in the same way.

To work a wrapped stitch purlwise, insert the right needle under the wrap from behind and then into the stitch (purlwise). Purl both the wrap and the stitch together.

The short rows add extra length to the center section of this collar stand. The wrapped stitches disguise the steps at the ends of the short rows.

188 **Planning short rows**

This diagram represents the short-row shaping for a collar stand.

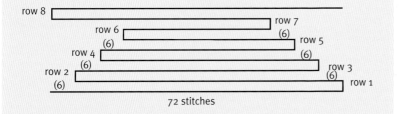

Beginning with 72 stitches, the collar is shaped as follows:
Row 1: K66 (to last 6 stitches), wrap the next stitch, turn.
Row 2: P60 (to last 6 stitches), wrap the next stitch, turn.
Row 3: K54 (to last 12 stitches), wrap the next stitch, turn.
Row 4: P48 (to last 12 stitches), wrap the next stitch, turn.
Row 5: K42 (to last 18 stitches), wrap the next stitch, turn.
Row 6: P36 (to last 18 stitches), wrap the next stitch, turn.
Row 7: K to the end, working knitwise into the wrapped stitches.
Row 8: P to the end, working purlwise into the remaining wrapped stitches (72 stitches).
Continue as required for the collar.

The body of this tote bag is worked in one piece. Graduated short rows increase the length of the knitting at the center to form the lower edge of the bag when the piece is folded in half.

At the back neck of this jacket, a stockinette-stitch collar stand has been worked just below the seed-stitch collar. The collar stand is shaped with short rows, using wrapped stitches to avoid holes in the work.

Lace and openwork stitches

Lacy patterns are formed by combining decreases (page 56) with yarn overs (page 54) to make extra stitches. In general, every decrease is balanced by a corresponding yarn over (or other increase). The arrangement of the decreases and increases, and the methods used to work them, determine the pattern.

Special abbreviations

K2tog = knit two together (page 56).
MB3 = make a 3-stitch bobble (page 93).
sl1p + slip 1 stitch purlwise (page 57).
ssk = slip, slip, knit (page 56).
s2togpo = slip two together knitwise, K1, pass slipped stitches over (page 59).
yo = yarn over to make an extra stitch (page 54).

192

Eyelet Stripes

Along the rows of eyelet holes, every double decrease is balanced by two yarn overs.
Requires a multiple of 4 stitches, plus 1.
Rows 1 & 2: K.
Row 3: P.
Rows 4 & 5: K.
Row 6 (wrong side row): P1, * yo, S2togpo, yo, P1, * repeat from * to * to the end.
Repeat these 6 rows, ending with row 1 or 4.

193

Eyelet Zigzags

Here, simple eyelets are arranged in zigzag formation. Requires a multiple of 8 stitches, plus 1.
Row 1: * K4, K2tog, yo, K2, * repeat from * to * to the last stitch, K1.
Row 2 and every wrong side row: P.
Row 3: * K3, K2tog, yo, K3, * repeat from * to * to the last stitch, K1.
Row 5: * K2, K2tog, yo, K4, * repeat from * to * to the last stitch, K1.
Row 7: * K3, yo, ssk, K3, * repeat from * to * to the last stitch, K1.
Row 9: * K4, yo, ssk, K2, * repeat from * to * to the last stitch, K1.
Row 11: * K5, yo, ssk, K1, * repeat from * to * to the last stitch, K1.
(Row 12 as row 2).
Repeat these 12 rows, ending with row 6 or row 12.

FIX IT

189 *Losing your place when knitting lace stitches?*

Try a test swatch first in a smooth, firm yarn so you can see exactly how the pattern forms. After practicing a few rows, you'll be able to see at a glance which row you're knitting.

190 *Losing track when knitting motifs such as Flower Motif?*

Place a ring marker at either side of the panel of stitches (17 stitches for Flower Motif) and slip the markers on every row.

191 *Holes too big?*

If a lace pattern is too open for your purpose, try working make one (page 55) instead of yarn over to make the holes smaller.

194 Old Shale

For this pattern, each group of several decreases is balanced by a corresponding group of increases, forming gentle scallops across the work, hence its other name, Feather and Fan Stitch. It is suitable for edgings because it will not curl.

Requires a multiple of 12 stitches, plus 1.

Row 1: K1, * (K2tog) twice, (yo, K1) 3 times, yo, (ssk) twice, K1, * repeat from * to * to the end.

Row 2: K.

Repeat these 2 rows, ending with row 2.

195 Eyelet Twist

This softly draping stitch has a vertical emphasis.

Requires a multiple of 5 stitches, plus 3.

Row 1: * K3, yo, K2tog, * repeat from * to * to the last 3 stitches, K3.

Row 2: * P4, K1, * repeat from * to * to the last 3 stitches, P3.

Row 3: * K3, K2tog, yo, * repeat from * to * to the last 3 stitches, K3.

Row 4: P3, * K1, P4, * repeat from * to * to the end.

Repeat these 4 rows, ending with row 2 or 4.

196 Butterflies

This easy little pattern makes a suitable substitute for stockinette stitch.

Requires a multiple of 10 stitches, plus 7.

Row 1: K1, * K2tog, yo, K1, yo, ssk, K5, * repeat from * to * to the last 6 stitches, K2tog, yo, K1, yo, ssk, K1.

Row 2: P3, * sl1p, P9, * repeat from * to * to last 4 stitches, sl1p, P3.

Rows 3 and 4: as rows 1 and 2.

Row 5: K1, * K5, K2tog, yo, K1, yo, ssk, * repeat from * to * to the last 6 stitches, K6.

Row 6: P8, * sl1p, P9, * repeat from * to * to the last 9 stitches, sl1p, P8.

Rows 7 and 8: as rows 5 and 6.

Repeat these 8 rows, ending with row 4 or 8.

197 Flower Motif

Eyelets and a bobble are used to form a little flower motif.

Place it wherever you wish, or repeat to form a border.

Requires a panel of 17 stitches.

Row 1: K5, K2tog, (K1, yo) twice, K1, ssk, K5.

Row 2 and every wrong side row: P.

Row 3: K4, K2tog, K1, yo, K3, yo, K1, ssk, K4.

Row 5: K3, K2tog, K1, yo, K5, yo, K1, ssk, K3.

Row 7: K2, (K2tog, K1, yo) twice, K1, (yo, K1, ssk) twice, K2.

Row 9: K1, (K2tog, K1, yo) twice, K3, (yo, K1, ssk) twice, K1.

Row 11: K3, K2tog, K1, yo, K5, yo, K1, ssk, K3.

Row 13: K5, yo, ssk, K1, MB3, K1, K2tog, yo, K5.

Row 15: K6, yo, ssk, K1, K2tog, yo, K6.

Row 17: K7, yo, s2togpo, yo, K7.

(Row 18 as row 2).

⊙ TRY IT

198 Variations

The reverse side of Eyelet Stripes can be used as the right side.

Try Old Shale in two-row stripes (page 53), or work the wrong-side row as a purl row to make a softer, more flexible fabric.

Cables and twists

Cables and twists add texture to a knitted garment and are much easier to knit than they first appear. Cables are formed by working the stitches out of order with the aid of a cable needle (page 13). Twists are worked over just two stitches, and no cable needle is required.

199 Cables

Cables may be worked over any reasonable number of stitches. Usually, half the stitches are slipped purlwise onto a cable needle and held at the front or back of the work. The second group of cable stitches is then worked, followed by the group from the cable needle. The numbers of stitches, and the order of their working, determine the formation of the cable pattern.

Working a cable twisted to the left

For a six-stitch cable as shown (abbreviation C6L, or C6F), slip 3 stitches purlwise onto the cable needle and hold at the front of the work. Knit the next 3 stitches, and then knit the 3 stitches from the cable needle.

Working a cable twisted to the right

For a six-stitch cable (abbreviation C6R or C6B), slip 3 stitches purlwise onto the cable needle and hold at the back of the work. Knit the next 3 stitches, and then knit the 3 from the cable needle.

200 Twists

Twists are pairs of stitches worked to give the appearance of twisting either to left or right, like little two-stitch cables. But instead of working a two-stitch cable in the manner described above, the following methods are used because they are much quicker and give a similar result.

Working a twist to the left (Twl)

1 | Skip the first stitch and knit into the back of the second stitch, leaving it on the left-hand needle.

2 | Now knit the first and second stitches together through the back loops, and slip both stitches off the left-hand needle.

◉TRY IT

201 Create added texture

Combine cable patterns with bobble patterns (page 92), twists, or other textures such as seed stitch.

Working a twist to the right (TwR)

1 | Knit two stitches together, leaving them on the left-hand needle.

2 | Now knit the first stitch again in the usual way and slip both stitches off the left-hand needle.

FIX IT

202 *Want to add cables to a simple sweater or pillow?*

You will probably need to add extra stitches to the width of the work, because cables pull in the width. Work a small swatch with a cable and compare the gauge to find out how many extra stitches you need.

203 Twist Rib

Substitute this stitch for 2 x 2 rib (page 64) to add interest to welts and cuffs. Requires a multiple of 4 stitches, plus 2.
Row 1: * P2, TwR, * repeat from * to * to the last 2 stitches, P2.
Row 2: * K2, P2, * repeat from * to * to the last 2 stitches, K2.
Repeat these 2 rows.

Special abbreviations

C4L = cable 4 stitches to the left.
C6L = cable 6 stitches to the left, as explained opposite.
C4R = cable 4 stitches to the right.
C6R = cable 6 stitches to the right, as explained opposite.
TwL = left twist as explained opposite.
TwR = right twist as explained above.

204 Double Cable

Cables may be combined in various ways to make larger cables. Here, two 6-stitch cables, back-to-back, are bordered by purl stitches for extra emphasis.

Requires a panel of 16 stitches: shown here on a background of stockinette stitch.
Row 1: P2, K12, P2.
Row 2 and every wrong side row: K2, P12, K2.
Rows 3–6: repeat rows 1 and 2, twice more.
Row 7: P2, C6R, C6L, P2.
Row 8: as row 2.
Rows 9 and 10: as rows 1 and 2.
Repeat these 10 rows as required.

205 Honeycomb

Combining right- and left-twisting cables results in an all-over honeycomb pattern. A firm stitch suitable for outdoor wear or home accessories.
Requires a multiple of 8 stitches.
Row 1: K.
Row 2 and every wrong side row: P.
Row 3: * C4L, C4R, * repeat from * to * to end.
Row 5: K.
Row 7: * C4R, C4L, * repeat from * to * to end.
(row 8 as row 2).
Repeat these 8 rows, ending with row 4 or 8.

Knots and bobbles

Bobbles and bold knots are made by working several stitches into one and then reducing the number of stitches back to one again before continuing along the row. Flat knots have a less raised structure, looking almost like tiny flowers.

Special abbreviations

FK = flat knot as explained below.
BK = bold knot as explained below.
K1tbl = knit one through back loop (page 58).
MB3 = 3-stitch bobble as explained opposite.
MB5 = 5-stitch bobble as explained opposite.
P1tbl = purl one through back loop (page 58).
P2tog = purl 2 together (page 57).
P3tog = purl 3 together (page 59).
s2togpo = slip 2 together, K1, pass slipped stitches over (page 59).
tbl = through back loop.
yo = yarn over (page 54).

⊚TRY IT

207 Bobble variations

• Substitute MB3 for MB5, or vice versa, in these patterns and others.
• Substitute bold knots for MB3 or MB5.
• Make bobbles more knobbly by working the wrong side row(s) of the bobble as K instead of P.
• Make bobbles larger by working two more rows on the 3 or 5 bobble stitches before decreasing down to 1 stitch.
• With practice, you can learn to purl the "P3" or "P5" of a bobble without turning the work, by pretending to be left-handed (if you are right-handed). It takes a little time to learn, but is well worth the effort if you want to knit a project with lots of bobbles.

206
Knots

Here are two ways to make little knots. Try them out and use whichever you prefer. The bold knot counts as one stitch, whereas the flat knot is worked over three stitches.

Making a bold knot (BK)

1 | Where the knot is required, use the two-needle method (page 44) to cast on 3 stitches.

2 | Knit the 3 new stitches and the next stitch, making 4 stitches on the right-hand needle.

3 | Lift the first three stitches, one at a time, over the fourth stitch to reduce the stitch number back down to one.

208
Flat Knots

Use this stitch as a substitute for stockinette stitch. Requires a multiple of 8 stitches, plus 1.
Row 1: * P1, K7, * repeat from * to * to the last stitch, P1.
Row 2: P.
Row 3: * P1, K2, FK, K2 * repeat from * to * to the last stitch, P1.
Row 4: P.
Repeat these 4 rows.

Making a flat knot (FK)

This knot is worked over 3 stitches: P3tog, yo, purl the same 3 stitches together again.

209

Bobbles

These are made by working several times into one stitch then working one or more rows on the new group of stitches and finally decreasing back down to one stitch.

Making a three-stitch bobble (MB3)

1 ❙ Knit into the front, back, and front of the required stitch, making 3 stitches from 1.

2 ❙ Turn the work and P3. Turn again, s2togpo. On the following row, push the bobble to the right side of the work and work the stitches to each side quite tightly.

Making a five-stitch bobble (MB5)

1 ❙ Work [K1, yo, K1, yo, K1] all into the required stitch.

2 ❙ Turn, P5. Turn, K5. Turn, P2tog, P1, P2tog. Turn, s2togpo.

210

Bobble Heart Motif

Bobbles of any size (or bold knots) can be used to form motifs, such as this heart worked on a background of stockinette stitch.
Requires a panel of 9 stitches.
Row 1: K4, MB3, K4.
Row 2 and every wrong side row: P.
Row 3: K3, MB3, K1, MB3, K3.
Row 5: K2, MB3, K3, MB3, K2.
Row 7: K1, MB3, K5, MB3, K1.
Row 9: MB3, K3, MB3, K3, MB3.
Row 11: MB3, K2, MB3, K1, MB3, K2, MB3.
Row 13: K1, MB3, K5, MB3, K1.
Continue in stockinette stitch.

211

Twist and Bobble Border

This makes an interesting border for stockinette stitch. Alternate stitches of the ribbing are worked through the back loops, making a firm single rib that will not curl.
Requires a multiple of 8 stitches, plus 3.
Row 1: * P1, K1tbl, * repeat from * to * to the last stitch, P1.
Row 2: * K1, P1tbl, * repeat from * to * the last stitch, K1.
Repeat these 2 rows twice more (or more times for a deeper border).
Row 3: * P1, MB5, [P1, K1tbl] 3 times, * repeat from * to * to the last 3 stitches, P1, MB5, P1.
Row 4: K3, * [P1tbl, K1] twice, P1tbl, K3, * repeat from * to * to the end.
Row 5: P1, * K1, P1, MB5, P1, K1tbl, P1, MB5, P1, * repeat from * to * to the last 2 stitches, K1, P1.
Row 6: K1, * P1, K3, P1tbl, K3, * repeat from * to * to the last 2 stitches, P1, K1.
Row 7: K3, * P2, MB5, P2, K3, * repeat from * to * to the end.
Row 8: P3, * K5, P3, * repeat from * to * to the end.
Row 9: K4, * P3, K5, * repeat from * to * to the last 7 stitches, P3, K4.
Row 10: P4, * K3, P5, * repeat from * to * to last the 7 stitches, K3, P5.
Row 11: K5, * P1, K7, * repeat from * to * to the last 6 stitches, P1, K5.
Row 12: P5, * K1, P7, * repeat from * to * to the last 6 stitches, K1, P5.
Continue in stockinette stitch.

Loops, leaves, and bells

The stitch numbers in these patterns do not remain constant from row to row. By increasing the stitches in various ways on one row, then decreasing them again on subsequent rows, bold shapes are formed that stand out in relief against the background.

Special abbreviations
K2tog = knit 2 together (page 56).
P2tog = purl 2 together (page 57).
ssk = slip, slip, knit (page 56).
s2togpo = slip 2 stitches together, K1, pass slipped stitches over (page 59).
yo = yarn over (page 54).
yo tw = yarn over twice (page 55)

212

Little Loops

The loops here are placed in vertical rows, but once you understand how they are made, you can add them to stockinette stitch in any arrangement you choose. Requires a multiple of 6 stitches.
Row 1: K.
Row 2: P.
Row 3: * K6, cast on 10 stitches, * repeat from * to * to last 6 stitches, K6.
Row 4: * P6, bind off next 9 stitches knitwise, * repeat from * to * to last 6 stitches, P6.
Row 5: K6, * pull the loop from the previous row to the front of the work, beneath the left-hand needle, K2tog, K5, * repeat from * to * to the end (making a multiple of 6 stitches).
Row 6: as row 2.
Repeat these 6 rows.

213

Leaves

Leaves here are arranged quite closely in a row, but you can place a single leaf, or several leaves, anywhere on your work. They show up best on a background of reverse stockinette stitch.
Requires a multiple of 6 stitches, plus 5. Begin with a few rows of reverse stockinette stitch, ending K row.
Row 1: * P5, K1, *, repeat from * to * to last 5 stitches, P5.
Rows 2, 4, 6, 8, 10, 12, 14, and 16: K the K stitches and purl the P stitches (and the yos) as they face you.
Row 3: * P5, yo, K1, yo, * repeat from * to * to the last 5 stitches, P5.
Row 5: * P5, K1, yo, K1, yo, K1, * repeat from * to * to the last 5 stitches, K5.
Row 7: * P5, K2, yo, K1, yo, K2, * repeat from * to * to the last 5 stitches, P5.
Rows 9 and 11: * P5, K7, * repeat from * to * to the last 5 stitches, P5.
Row 13: * P5, ssk, K3, K2tog, * repeat from * to * to the last 5 stitches, P5.
Row 15: * P5, ssk, K1, K2tog, * repeat from * to * to the last 5 stitches, P5.
Row 17: * P5, s2togpo, * repeat from * to * to the last 5 stitches, P5.
Row 18: K.
Continue in reverse stockinette stitch.

214

Row of Bells

As with the leaves, once you understand how the bells are formed, you can add a group of bells wherever you like on your work. Use the simple thumb cast-on method (page 45) to make the extra stitches on row 1.
Requires a multiple of 4 stitches. Begin with a few rows of reverse stockinette stitch, ending K row.
Row 1: * P4, cast on 7 stitches, * repeat from * to * to the last 4 stitches, P4.
Row 2: * K4, P7, * repeat from * to * to the last 4 stitches, K4.
Row 3: * P4, K7, * repeat from * to * to the last 4 stitches, P4.
Rows 4, 6, 8 and 10: K the K stitches and P the P stitches as they face you.
Row 5: * P4, ssk, K3, K2tog, * repeat from * to * to the last 4 stitches, P4.
Row 7: * P4, ssk, K1, K2tog, * repeat from * to * to the last 4 stitches, P4.
Row 9: * P4, s2togpo, * repeat from * to * to the last 4 stitches, P4.
Row 11: * P3, P2tog, * repeat from * to * to the last 4 stitches, P4.
Continue in reverse stockinette stitch.

⊚ TRY IT

215 **Make a frilled edge**

Cast on a multiple of 11 stitches plus 4, then work the Row of Bells from row 2 to the end. You'll end with a multiple of 4 stitches.

Edgings

These edgings are knitted sideways and are designed to lie flat without curling. Make them to the length you need then simply sew them in place. Alternatively, make the edging first then pick up stitches along one edge to work the main part of your project.

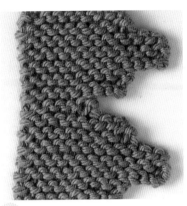

216

Stepped Edging

Cast on 6 stitches.
Rows 1 & 2: K.
Row 3: Cast on 2 stitches, K to end.
Rows 4, 5 & 6: K.
Rows 7–10: as rows 3–6. You now have 10 stitches.
Row 11: Bind off 2 stitches, K to end.
Rows 12, 13 & 14: K.
Rows 15–18: as rows 11–14. 6 stitches.
Repeat rows 3–18.

217

Zigzag Edging

Cast on 6 stitches.
Row 1: K2, yo, K2tog, yo, K2.
Rows 2, 4, 6 and 8: K.
Row 3: K3, yo, K2tog, yo, K2.
Row 5: K4, yo, K2tog, yo, K2.
Row 7: K5, yo, K2tog, yo, K2.
Row 9: K6, yo, K2tog, yo, K2.
Row 10: Bind off 5 stitches, K to end.
Repeat these 10 rows.

218

Picot Edging

Cast on 6 stitches.
Row 1: K1, K2tog, yo, K2, yo twice, K1.
Row 2: K1, K into front and back of yo twice, K2tog, yo, K3.
Row 3: K1, K2tog, yo, K5.
Row 4: Bind off 2 stitches, K2tog, yo, K3.
Repeat these 4 rows.

⊚TRY IT

219 Knit to fit

When knitting an edging to match the length of a main piece, work to the length you think you need without binding off. Sew the edging in place and adjust the length to fit exactly before binding off the edging.

Chevron patterns

By placing increases in vertical lines, spaced apart from vertical lines of decreases, the knitted rows take up a zigzag formation. The holes created by yarn-over increases create an added lacy effect and additional patterns can be added between the increases and decreases as desired.

Special abbreviations
K2tog = knit 2 together (page 56).
P3tog = purl 3 together.
ssk = slip, slip, knit (page 56).
s2togpo = slip 2 stitches together, K1, pass slipped stitches over (page 59).
yo = yarn over (page 54).

220
Small Chevrons

Each double decrease in this pattern is balanced by two yarn over increases. If desired, the chevrons can be worked in two-row stripes (page 53) to emphasize the shape. Requires a multiple of 12 stitches, plus 1.
Row 1: * K1, yo, K4, s2togpo, K4, yo, * repeat from * to * to the last stitch, K1.
Row 2: P.
Repeat these 2 rows.

221
Large Chevrons

This chevron uses two paired decreases instead of the double decrease used for the small chevron pattern, so it's useful to place a ring marker at the center to remind you when to decrease. Suits any even number of stitches (36 shown here):
Row 1: K1, yo, K to the center 4 stitches (2 stitches before the marker), ssk, K2tog, K to the last stitch, yo, K1.
Row 2: P.
Repeat these 2 rows. Slip the marker on every row.

⊚TRY IT

222 **Make it firmer**

Work the wrong-side rows of a chevron pattern as knit instead of purl to make a firmer fabric with added texture.

This sweater is worked throughout in chevrons. The number of stitches between the increase and decreases was carefully chosen to suit the shaping required at neck and armhole. The shade-dyed yarn highlights the zigzag formation with subtle stripes of color.

223 Lace Chevron

Textures may be added to chevron patterns by working the stitches between the increases and decreases in different ways, such as the eyelet holes shown here.

Requires a multiple of 16 stitches, plus 1.

Row 1: * K1, yo, K6, s2togpo, K6, yo, * repeat from * to * to the last stitch, K1.

Row 2: P.

Row 3: * K1, yo, [ssk, yo] 3 times, s2togpo, [yo, K2tog] 3 times, yo, * repeat from * to * to the last stitch, K1.

Row 4: P.

Row 5: as row 1.

Row 6: * P1, K7, * repeat from * to * to the last stitch, P1.

Repeat these 6 rows.

224 Chevron and Leaf Border

Use this border instead of ribbing at the lower edge of knitting. The shaping forming the leaves cancels out the zigzag formation of the chevrons so the work can continue in stockinette stitch.

Requires a multiple of 14 stitches, plus 1.

Row 1: * K1, yo, P5, P3tog, P5, yo, * repeat from * to * to the last stitch, K1.

Row 2 and every wrong side row: P.

Repeat these 2 rows 5 more times (or more for a deeper chevron).

Row 13: * K1, yo, ssk, yo, P3, P3tog, P3, yo, K2tog, yo, * repeat from * to * to the last stitch, K1.

Row 15: * K1, yo, K1, ssk, yo, P2, P3tog, P2, yo, K2tog, K1, yo, * repeat from * to * to the last stitch, K1.

Row 17: * K1, yo, K2, ssk, yo, P1, P3tog, P1, yo, K2tog, K2, yo, * repeat from * to * to the last stitch, K1.

Row 19: * K1, yo, K3, ssk, yo, P3tog, yo, K2tog, K3, yo, * repeat from * to * to the last stitch, K1.

Row 21: * K4, K2tog, yo, K3, yo, ssk, K3, * repeat from * to * to the last stitch, K1.

Row 23: * K3, K2tog, yo, K5, yo, ssk, K2, * repeat from * to * to the last stitch, K1.

Row 25: * K2, K2tog, yo, K7, yo, ssk, K1, * repeat from * to * to the last stitch, K1.

Row 27: * K1, K2tog, yo, K9, yo, ssk, * repeat from * to * to the last stitch, K1.

Row 29: K2tog, yo, * K 11, yo, P3tog, yo, * repeat from * to * to the last 13 stitches, K11, yo, ssk.

Continue in stockinette stitch (beginning P row).

FIX IT

 225 *Don't know how to gauge a chevron pattern?*

Lay a stitch sample flat and measure the width straight across, (not following the zigzag formation).

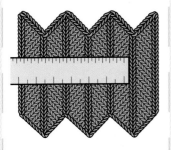

⊚TRY IT

 226 Alternative increases

Increases may be made by m1 (for a smaller hole), or by the invisible increase, m1 tbl (page 55) instead of the yo method used here.

Patchwork squares

Knitted squares can be stitched together to make patchwork blankets, pillows, tote bags, and other articles, including clothing. It is a great way to use up yarn remnants. Squares made in garter stitch keep their shape in use, and make a firm fabric that will last for years. Two ways to knit garter-stitch squares are given here.

Special abbreviations

Ktw = knit twice into same stitch (page 54).
K2tog = knit 2 together (page 56).
P2tog = purl 2 together (page 57).
P3tog = purl 3 together (page 59).
ssk = slip, slip, knit (page 56).

227 Knitting a corner-to-corner square

Using the needle size recommended for your yarn, cast on 2 stitches.
Row 1: Ktw, K1. You now have 3 stitches.
Row 2: Ktw, K to end.
Repeat row 2 until the side edges measure the length you want—4in (10cm) or 6in (15cm), for example. Finish with an even number of stitches, so you have worked an even number of rows. This example was increased to 24 stitches.
Next row: K2tog, K to end.
Repeat this row until 2 stitches remain. You have worked an even number of decreasing rows.
Lift the first stitch over the second and off the needle. Bind off.

228 Knitting a decreasing square

Decide how many stitches you need for one side of the square: here, 18 stitches in worsted yarn = about 4in (10cm). Cast on twice this number (36 stitches in the example).
Row 1: K to the center, place a ring marker, K to end.
Row 2 (right side row): K to 2 stitches before the marker, K2tog, slip the marker, ssk, K to end.
Row 3 (wrong side row): K, slipping marker. (To help keep track of the rows, place a safety pin on the right side of the work.) Repeat rows 2 and 3 until 4 stitches remain, ending with row 3.
Last row: K2tog, remove the marker, ssk. Bind off the remaining 2 stitches.

Identically striped corner-to-corner squares may be arranged to form various geometric patterns. Join squares with the ladder stitch seam (page 140).

Decreasing squares with striped patterns may be joined together to create more intricate designs. In this case, the stripes were added to the first few rows only.

⊚ TRY IT

229 Make a baby blanket

Make lots of square using remnants of yarns in different colors but of similar weights and join them together into a baby blanket. The whole thing can be unified with a simple crochet border.

Entrelac

Entrelac knitting is a fascinating way of producing a patchwork effect, knitted all in one piece without seams. You can use one or more yarn colors, or experiment with space-dyed yarns.

The changing direction of the blocks in entrelac knitting gives the appearance of strips of knitting, woven together.

230 Working entrelac

The instructions below are based on a block size of 10 stitches by 20 rows. You can choose any number of stitches for your blocks; the number of rows in each block will always be twice the number of stitches. Use the needle size recommended for your yarn. Changing color for each row of blocks will help you understand the method.

Knitting the base triangles

Using the first color, cast on a multiple of 10 stitches (40 stitches shown here).
1st base triangle: P2, turn, K2, turn, P3, turn, K3, turn. Continue in this way, purling 1 more stitch from the left-hand needle on every alternate row until there are 10 stitches on the right-hand needle. Do not turn. Leave these 10 stitches on the needle.
2nd and following base triangles: Work as for 1st base triangle.

Working the first row of blocks

The first row of blocks begins (and ends) with a side triangle.
Change to the second color.
1st side triangle: K2, turn, P2, turn, Ktw, ssk, turn, P3, turn, Ktw, K1, ssk, turn, P4, turn. Continue in this way until the row "Ktw, K7, ssk" has been worked. Do not turn. Leave these 10 stitches on the needle.
Block: Pick up and knit 10 stitches from the side edge of the base triangle (1 stitch from every alt row). Turn, P10, turn. * K9, ssk, turn, P10*, repeat from * to * until all 10 stitches of the next base triangle have been decreased. Do not turn.
Repeat this block in all the spaces between the base triangles.
2nd side triangle: Pick up and knit 10 stitches from the side edge of the last base triangle, turn, P2tog, P8, turn, K9, turn. P2tog, P7, turn, K8. Continue in this way until 1 stitch remains. Turn and slip this stitch onto the left-hand needle.

Working the second row of blocks

The second row of blocks has no side triangles.
Change back to the first color.
Block: P1, pick up and purl 9 stitches from the side edge of the previous side triangle, turn, K10, turn. * P9, P2tog, turn, K10 *, repeat from * to * until all 10 stitches of the next block have been decreased. Do not turn.
Begin the 2nd and following blocks by picking up and purling 10 stitches from the side edge of the next block, then work the new block in the same way.

Working the final row of triangles

This last row of triangles makes a straight edge at the top of the work.
Change to the first color.
1st triangle: P1, pick up and purl 9 stitches from the side edge of the side triangle, turn, K10, turn. P2tog, P7, P2tog, turn, K9, turn. P2tog, P6, P2tog, turn, K8, turn. Continue in this way until turn, K2 has been worked. Turn, P1, P2tog, turn, K2, turn, P3tog. 1 stitch remains.
2nd triangle: Pick up and purl 9 stitches from the side edge of the next block and then complete the triangle in the same way as the first triangle.
Repeat the 2nd triangle to the end of the row.

Frills and flutes

Frills are flared knitted sections, wider on one edge than the other, while a flute is a frill that has been worked in a ribbed design, placing the shaping carefully so that the ribs widen towards the outer edge. Frills may be constructed in a number of ways, but for a satisfactory result the outer edge needs to be at least three or four times longer than the inner edge.

Special abbreviations

K2tog = knit two together (page 56).
P2tog = purl 2 together (page 57).
sl1p = slip 1 purlwise (page 57).
ssk = slip, slip, knit (page 56).
s2togpo = slip 2 together, K1, pass slipped stitches over (page 59).
yo = yarn over (page 54).

232

Making a decreasing frill

This frill begins at the outer edge and may be used as a ribbing substitute. Use the same size needles as for the main part of the work to cast on 4 times the number of stitches required at the top of the frill, plus 1. Using the long-tail cast-on (page 43) gives the best result.
Row 1: K1, * K2, lift the first of these 2 stitches over the second stitch and off the needle, * repeat from * to * to the end.
Row 2: P1, * P2tog, * repeat from * to * to the end.
Number of stitches remaining = number required, plus 1. Decrease the extra stitch on the next row to work the main part of the knitting.

233

Making an increasing frill

This frill is worked outward from the inner edge, increasing by the yarn-over method (page 54). It is shown here worked along the top edge of a piece of stockinette stitch. You can also work this frill by picking up and knitting stitches from any edge required.
Begin with any number of stitches.
Row 1: * K1, yo, * repeat from * to * to the last stitch, K1.
Row 2: * P1, yo, * repeat from * to * to the last stitch, P1.
Bind off loosely using a needle one or two sizes larger.

234

Working a chevron frill

This frill begins at the outer edge. By using the double decrease (page 59), the cast-on edge is pulled into a zigzag. This frill "grows" neatly into a 1 x 1 rib.
Cast on 3 times the number of stitches required at the top of the frill, adjusting the total to a multiple of 6 stitches, plus 1.
Row 1: P1, * yo, K1, s2togpo, K1, yo, P1 * repeat from * to * to the end.
Row 2: K1, * P5, K1, * repeat from * to * to the end.
Rows 3 & 4: As rows 1 & 2.
Row 5: P1, * K1, s2togpo, K1, P1, * repeat from * to * to the end.
Row 6: K1, * P3, K1, * repeat from * to * to the end.
Row 7: P1, * s2togpo, P1, * repeat from * to * to the end.
Row 8: K1, * P1, K1, * repeat from * to * to the end.

FIX IT

235 *Too many stitches?*
For really long frills, use a circular needle to hold all the stitches easily.

236 Working a sideways frill

This frill is knitted sideways using the short-row technique, and may be made to any length, then sewn in place using a ladder stitch seam (page 140). The outer edge is finished with a chain selvage, and the inner edge with a garter stitch selvage, to be taken into the seam.
Cast on 10 stitches.
Row 1: Sl1p, K3, turn.
Row 2: P3, K1.
Row 3: Sl1p, K6, turn.
Row 4: P6, K1.
Row 5: Sl1p, K9.
Row 6: K10.
Row 7: Sl1p, P3, turn.
Row 8: K4.
Row 9: Sl1p, P6, turn.
Row 10: K7.
Row 11: Sl1p, P8, K1.
Row 12: K1, P8, K1.
Repeat these 12 rows to length required.

237 Working a fluted frill

This frill begins at the outer edge. By pairing the decreases, bell-shaped "flutes" are formed.
For every 3 stitches required at the top of the frill, cast on 7 stitches; add 2 more.
Row 1: P2, * K5, P2, * repeat from * to * to the end.
Row 2: K2, * P5, K2, * repeat from * to * to the end.
Rows 3 & 4: as rows 1 & 2.
Row 5: P2, * ssk, K1, K2tog, P2, * repeat from * to * to the end.
Row 6: K2, * P3, K2, * repeat from * to * to the end.
Row 7: P2, * K3, P2, * repeat from * to * to the end.
Row 8: as row 6.
Row 9: P2, * s2togpo, P2, * repeat from * to * to the end.
Row 10: K2, * P1, K2, * repeat from * to * to the end.

238 Ribbed frill

This frill is knitted outward, increasing toward the outer edge. This sleeve was knitted first, beginning with a provisional cast-on, then the stitches for the frill were picked up and knitted downward.
Begin with an even number of stitches.
Rows 1–4: *K1, P1, * repeat from * to * to the end.
Row 5: * [K1, P1, K1] all into the same stitch, P1, * repeat from * to * to the end.
Row 6: as row 1.
Row 7: as row 5.
Row 8: as row 1. Number of stitches = 4 x number on row 1.
Bind off loosely in rib as set. Changing to a contrast color for the bind-off adds emphasis to the frill.

⊚TRY IT

239 Adjust the frill length

The chevron and fluted frills may be made longer by working more unshaped rows between the decreasing rows.

240 Add a frill anywhere

To add a frill across a piece of knitting (i.e. not along an edge), work a row of purl stitches where the top of the frill is required and complete the piece. Then pick up stitches from the purl row and work the increasing frill (opposite) or ribbed frill (below).

KNITTING IN THE ROUND

Circular knitting or "knitting in the round" is a fascinating form of knitting: seamless garments and accessories of all kinds may be constructed from three-dimensional, tubular shapes. Such garments have no bulky seams and no weak points; they flex with the body completely, and are therefore very comfortable and practical.

Circular knitting

Why knit in the round?

With circular knitting, the work is not made in rows, but knitted around and around the needle(s) in a continuous spiral. This means that you can create a seamless sleeve or bag, for example. The right side of the work is always facing you, making two-color patterns and textured stitches easy to follow.

241

Choosing needles

Circular knitting is made on a circular needle or on a set of four (or sometimes five) double-pointed needles. Choose the correct option for your work in progress: a circular needle might be the best choice for the body of a sweater, while smaller pieces, such as a sleeve or neckband, might be best worked on double-pointed needles.

Circular needles

To knit a tube with a circumference of 16in (40cm) or more, a circular needle is the easiest option to handle. Circular needles are made with a flexible center section (usually nylon) and a rigid tip at each end. They are available in the usual range of sizes, and also in various lengths from 12in (30cm) up to 36in (90cm) or more.
Needle size, as with standard knitting needles, should suit the chosen yarn.
Needle length should be 4in (10cm) or more shorter than the circumference of the piece to be knitted: a circular needle will accommodate stitches equivalent to approximately twice its length. A circular needle that is too long for the number of stitches will stretch the knitting, and the stitches will not easily slip around it, making the knitting process difficult.

Double-pointed needles (dpn)

Double-pointed needles are the correct choice for small tubes. They may also be used to knit tubes of any size, although if the technique is unfamiliar, you may find them rather trickier to handle than a circular needle.
Double-pointed needles are available in the usual range of sizes, and in various lengths from 6in (15cm) up to 14in (35cm) or more. Sets normally consist of four or five needles.
Needle size, as with standard knitting needles, should suit the chosen yarn.
Needle length must be long enough to easily hold one-third of the required stitches (to work on four needles), or one-quarter (to work on five needles).
If the needles are too short the stitches will tend to drop off the tips. It is perfectly possible to knit even tiny tubes on long-length double-pointed needles, although shorter ones are more convenient.

Interchangeable needles

A kit of interchangeable tips and cords may be used to assemble circular needles of various sizes and lengths, to suit your project (page 11).

◉TRY IT

242 **Smooth cast-on**

To make a smooth cast-on edge, without a little step where the first round begins, cast on one more stitch than required. Arrange the circular needle or set of double-pointed needles ready to work the first round and then slip the first stitch from the left needle onto the right needle. Lift the next stitch on the right needle over the slipped stitch.

243

Working circular knitting

The basic techniques used for flat knitting are adapted in various ways for circular knitting.

Casting on with a circular needle

2 | Make sure that the cast-on edge is not twisted around the needle like this, or the knitting will be twisted too.

1 | Use the two needle tips as you would a pair of ordinary needles. Cast on the required number of stitches. Lay the needle on a flat surface with the tips away from you and the tip with the working yarn on the right. Arrange the stitches evenly around the needle with the cast-on edge to the inside all around.

Working a round on circular needles

To mark the beginning/end of the round, slip a ring marker onto the right needle tip. Knit or purl the stitches as required. Every few stitches, push more stitches to be worked up the left needle tip, and push the new stitches away from the right needle tip, so all the stitches slip around the flexible cord. When you reach the marker again, one round is complete. Slip the marker and begin the next round.

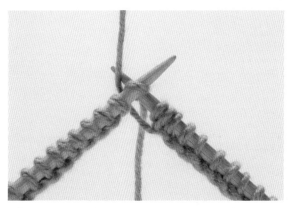

3 | Pick up the needle, lifting the needle tips toward you. The tip with the working yarn should be on the right. The yarn itself should lie loosely outside the circle, not down through the center. Hold needle tips according to your chosen method.

Casting on for double-pointed needles

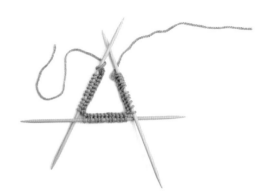

1 Depending on the cast-on method chosen, you will need one (or two) needles of the same size as the double-pointed needles, long enough to hold all the required stitches. (Use ordinary straight needles or a circular needle.) Using one of the methods, cast the required stitches onto one long needle. Slip one-third of the stitches purlwise onto one of the double-pointed needles.

2 Slip the remaining two-thirds of the stitches onto two more double-pointed needles. Some pattern instructions may require an exact number of stitches on each needle; otherwise, just divide the stitches into thirds. Arrange the needles in a triangle, so that the working yarn is at top right. The cast-on edge should be inside the triangle all around. Push each group of stitches toward the center of each needle. The leading tip of each needle (working counter-clockwise) should overlap the next needle.

Working a round on double-pointed needles

Working with five needles

1 Pick up the work, bringing the needle tips with the working yarn toward you. The working yarn should be outside the triangle, not down through the center. Use the fourth needle to knit or purl all the stitches on the first needle, as required. Bunch the new stitches together at the center of the fourth needle. The first needle is now empty; use it to work the stitches on the second needle, and so on.

2 Work the first and last stitches on each needle quite tightly and keeping the needles close together to prevent gaps caused by loose stitches. To mark the beginning/end of the round, place a ring marker one stitch from the end of the last needle, i.e. one stitch from the end of the round (otherwise it will fall off). Slip the ring marker on every round.

Sometimes it is more convenient to work on a set of five needles. In this case, divide the stitches evenly between four of the needles and use the fifth needle to begin the round.

Calculating the gauge

Gauge (page 20) is affected by the exact type of needles you use and the way you hold them, so it is important to check your circular gauge by knitting a tube — a flat sample piece, even on the same needle(s), may not exactly match your circular gauge.

Cast on enough stitches to comfortably fill the circular needle. For double-pointed needles, cast on enough stitches for a circumference of 10in (25cm). Work in the desired stitch for 6in (15cm). There is no need to bind off; slip the stitches onto a length of contrasting yarn. Block the sample appropriately. Now lay the sample flat and measure the gauge.

Alternatively, you can begin a project such as a sweater by knitting a small part, such as half a sleeve. Slip the stitches (purlwise) off the needles onto a length of contrasting yarn and measure the gauge as left. If the gauge is correct, slip the stitches (purlwise) back onto the needles and continue knitting; if the gauge is wrong, you need to begin again.

Stitch patterns for circular knitting

Stitch patterns of all kinds may be worked in circular knitting but because there are no wrong side rows, the methods of working them are rather different. The same principles apply whether you are using a circular needle or a set of double-pointed needles.

244 Basic stitches

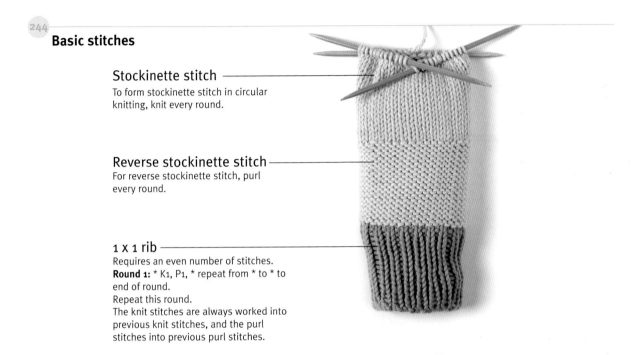

Stockinette stitch
To form stockinette stitch in circular knitting, knit every round.

Reverse stockinette stitch
For reverse stockinette stitch, purl every round.

1 x 1 rib
Requires an even number of stitches.
Round 1: * K1, P1, * repeat from * to * to end of round.
Repeat this round.
The knit stitches are always worked into previous knit stitches, and the purl stitches into previous purl stitches.

Garter stitch
In flat knitting, garter stitch is formed by knitting both right- and wrong-side rows. To match this construction in circular knitting work as follows:
Round 1: Knit to end.
Round 2: Purl to end.
Repeat these 2 rounds.

2 x 2 rib
Various ribs, such as 2 x 2 rib (requiring a multiple of 4 stitches), may be worked on the same principle as the 1 x 1 rib shown opposite:
Round 1: * K2, P2, * repeat from * to * to end.
Repeat this round.

245 Counting rounds

A counter is a useful accessory for keeping track of rounds because the normal type of row tally (which slips onto a straight needle) cannot be used. Every time you reach the ring marker at the end of a round, simply press the top of the counter to add to the tally of rows. (Otherwise, keep a slip of paper and pencil handy to keep a record of the rounds as you complete them.)

Special abbreviations

1A = knit 1 in yarn A.
1B = knit 1 in yarn B.
C6L = cable 6 stitches to the left (page 90).
C6R = cable 6 stitches to the right (page 90).
K2tog = knit 2 together (page 56).
s2togpo = vertical double decrease (page 59).
ssk = slip, slip, knit (page 56).
yo = yarn over (page 54).

246

Textured stitches

Instructions for textured stitches, such as cables, knots, and lace patterns are normally written for flat knitting in rows. The patterning is most often worked on the right-side rows, with the wrong-side rows worked quite simply in purl stitches or a combination of knit and purl. Once you understand how to convert a wrong-side row into a round, you can figure out how to work these patterns in circular knitting. Always use a marker to indicate the beginning/end of each round.

Repeating stitch patterns for circular knitting should never include the one or more extra stitches that may be necessary to balance the pattern in flat knitting. For circular knitting, the number of stitches in use should always divide exactly by the number in the repeat.

247

248

249

Eyelet Zigzags

Instructions for working this pattern in rows are on page 88. Compare them with the instructions below, for working the same pattern in rounds: instead of working a wrong-side row of purl stitches, you need to work a plain round of knit stitches.
Requires a multiple of 8 stitches. (No extra stitch is required to balance the pattern).
Round 1: * K4, K2tog, yo, K2, * repeat from * to * to end.
Round 2 and every alternate round: K (instead of P).
Round 3: * K3, K2tog, yo, K3, * repeat from * to * to end.
Round 5: * K2, K2tog, yo, K4, * repeat from * to * to end.
Round 7: * K3, yo, ssk, K3, * repeat from * to * to end.
Round 9: * K4, yo, ssk, K2, * repeat from * to * to end.
Round 11: * K5, yo, ssk, K1, * repeat from * to * to end.
(Round 12 as round 2).
Repeat these 12 rounds, ending with round 6 or round 12.

Double Cable

This is the cable described on page 91, but with the instructions adapted for circular knitting. In the original instructions, wrong-side rows are worked with knit and purl stitches to make a little rib at either side of the cable. To make the corresponding alternate rounds in circular knitting, the purl and knit stitches are reversed because the right side of the work is facing you.
Requires a panel of 16 stitches: shown here on a background of stockinette stitch (all rounds K). Place a ring marker at each side of the 16 cable panel stitches (use a different color to the marker at the beginning/end of the round). If you are working on double-pointed needles, arrange the stitches (by slipping them purlwise) so that all the panel stitches are on the same needle.
Work the 16 stitches between the new markers as follows:
Round 1: P2, K12, P2.
Round 2 and every alternate round: P2, K12, P2 (instead of K2, P12, K2).
Rounds 3–6: repeat rounds 1 and 2, twice more.
Round 7: P2, C6R, C6L, P2.
Round 8: as round 2.
Rounds 9 and 10: as rounds 1 and 2.
Repeat these 10 rounds as required.

Lace Chevron

The instructions for this stitch pattern in flat knitting appear on page 97. For circular knitting, adapt the pattern as explained here.
Requires a multiple of 16 stitches (no extra stitch required to balance the edges). If you are working on double-pointed needles, slip the stitches purlwise to arrange a multiple of 16 stitches on each needle.
Round 1: * K1, yo, K6, S2togpo, K6, yo, * repeat from * to * to end.
Round 2: K (instead of P).
Round 3: * K1, yo, [ssk, yo] 3 times, S2togpo, [yo, K2tog] 3 times, yo, * repeat from * to * to end.
Round 4: K (instead of P).
Round 5: as row 1.
Round 6: * K1, P7, * repeat from * to * to end. (Instead of P1, K7).
Repeat these 6 rounds.

250
Two-color knitting

This technique is particularly suitable for circular knitting because it is easy to keep the pattern correct when the right side of the work is always facing you. Also, such patterns are normally worked in stockinette stitch, so in circular knitting all rounds are knitted.

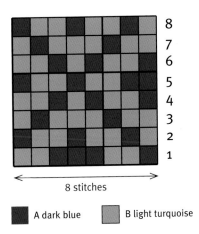

8 stitches

■ A dark blue   ■ B light turquoise

Reading from a chart

For circular knitting, every line of a chart is read from right to left. Above is the same chart as shown on page 122, adapted for circular knitting. The circular-knit version requires a multiple of 8 stitches, with no extra stitch to balance the pattern. All the rounds are numbered on the right.

Knitting from a two-color chart

Use a ring marker to indicate the beginning/end of each round. All the rounds are worked knitwise. All chart rows are read from right to left. This sample is worked as follows:
Round 1: K * 1A, 2B, 3A, 2B *, repeat from * to * to the end.
Round 2: K * 1B, 1A, 2B, 1A, 2B, 1A *, repeat from * to * to the end.
Continue in this way reading from successive chart rows and repeating the 8 rounds as required.

251
Mark the repeats

For a complicated two-color pattern with a large number of stitches to be repeated, place a ring marker on the needle(s) between each repeat.

252
Visible step between rounds?

Try to position the beginning/end of the rounds in an unobtrusive place: at the underarm on the body or sleeve of a sweater, or at center back on a yoke or hat. As a garment is washed and worn, the step will become less noticeable.

Dealing with floats

Long strands of yarn "floated" across the wrong side of the work may be dealt with by stranding, weaving, or twisting, as described on pages 122–123. Follow the instructions for working these techniques on a right-side (K) row.

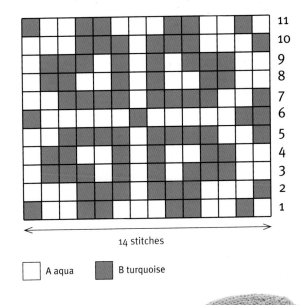

14 stitches

□ A aqua   ■ B turquoise

This two-color pattern band requires stranding; no color is carried behind more than five stitches on any chart row, so weaving or twisting the floats is not necessary provided that they are left loose enough to enable the work to lie flat.

253
Want to place a single motif on a circular knit?

Intarsia designs are rarely used with circular knitting because after knitting the first round, all the tails of color are in the wrong place for knitting the second round. Small designs may be adapted by working them in duplicate stitch (page 126) on a plain background. For a larger design, work the garment section in flat knitting, with one or two seams placed unobtrusively.

Circular knitted shapes

Circular knitting can be adapted to make seamless tubes of all sizes, or shaped with darts (page 84) to make cones, rounded domes, or flat circles.

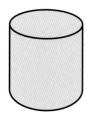 Straight tubes may be made to any size using circular needles for large sizes and sets of double-pointed needles for smaller sizes.

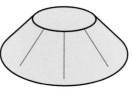 Tapered tubes may be increased (or decreased) at one side (e.g. for a sleeve), or evenly all around at intervals.

 A shallow cone (e.g. for a sweater yoke) is usually worked with evenly spaced dart shaping.

 A dome (e.g. for a hat) is also shaped with darts, decreasing more sharply toward the center top.

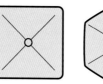 Flat medallions may be worked from the center outward in various geometric shapes.

254

Neckbands

Circular knitting makes a great neckband with no seam for a sweater. Use a circular needle shorter in length than the circumference of the neck opening, or a set of double-pointed needles. Pick up stitches around the neck opening and work in rib or another suitable stitch for the length required. The simple roll neck shown here is worked as a tube of stockinette, which naturally rolls over, purl side out, with no ugly seam.

255

Sweaters

Yoke in 8 sections

Sleeve

Sleeve

Body

The yoke of this sweater is shaped with eight darts (page 85). A collar stand (page 73) is added at the back to make the back neck length deeper than the front.

A circular-knit sweater may be constructed from a large tube for the body and two tapered tubes for the sleeves, joined into a single large cone for the yoke. Note that at each underarm, a group of stitches (about 2in (5cm) wide) is left on a holder on each sleeve, with a corresponding group left at each side of the body. Stitches for the yoke are picked up omitting these groups, which are later joined by grafting or binding off together (pages 144–146).

256

Hats

Circular knitting shaped with darts (page 84) makes cozy, well-fitting hats. The knitting may begin at the lower edge and the shaping is formed by decreasing at the darts. At first, the darts are decreased on every fourth or sixth round. Toward the center top, work decrease rounds more frequently to gather the top in sharply— otherwise the top will come to a point.

The top of this hat is shaped with six darts, using paired decreases.

257

Medallions

Medallions are flat, geometric shapes knitted on four or five double-pointed needles, beginning at the center. Two large medallions will make a pillow, two smaller medallions a purse. Or, you can construct a hat by beginning with a medallion and increasing up to the required circumference, then work the sides as a tube to the depth required.

Square medallion

Cast on 8 sts and arrange 2 sts on each of 4 needles from a set of five.
Round 1: K through back loops.
Round 2: on each needle: K1, m1, K1. 12 sts.
Round 3: K.
Round 4: on each needle: K1, m1, K1, m1, K1. 20 sts.
Round 5: K.
Round 6: on each needle: K1, m1, K to last st, m1, K1. 28 sts. Repeat rounds 5 and 6 to size required. 8 sts are increased on every alternate round.

Square with spiral increasing

Cast on 8 sts and arrange 2 sts on each of 4 needles from a set of five.
Round 1: K through back loops.
Round 2: on each needle: Yo, K to end. 12 sts. Repeat round 2 to size required. 4 sts are increased on every round.

Hexagon

Cast on 12 sts and arrange 4 sts on each of 3 needles from a set of 4.
Round 1: K through back loops.
Round 2: on each needle: [yo, K2] twice. 18 sts.
Round 3: K.
Round 4: on each needle: [yo, K3] twice. 24 sts.
Round 5: K.
Round 6: on each needle: [yo, K4] twice. 30 sts. Continue in this way working 1 extra st between yos on every alternate round, up to the size required. 6 sts are increased on every alternate round.

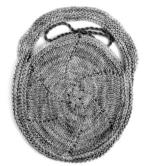

This little purse in hand-dyed silk is made of two hexagons, with a strip of garter stitch for the gusset and handle.

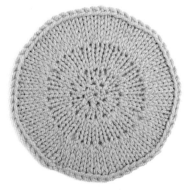

Radiating circle

Cast on 8 sts and arrange 2 sts on each of 4 needles from a set of five.
Round 1: K through back loops.
Round 2: on each needle: * m1, K1, * repeat from * to * to end. 16 sts.
Rounds 3, 4 & 5: K.
Round 6: as round 2. 32 sts.
Rounds 7, 8, 9,10 & 11: K.
Repeat last 6 rounds to size required. Number of stitches doubles on next and every foll 6th round. For a more open effect, use yo increase instead of m1.

◎TRY IT

258 **Make a patchwork**

Make lots of small medallions and join them to make a patchwork throw or cute little baby blanket.

Mittens and gloves

Small tubes like those used to construct mittens and gloves
are worked on double-pointed needles to avoid seams.

259
Ensuring accuracy

Measurements for gloves and mittens need to be accurate to ensure a good
fit. No ease is added to the measurements. Knit a swatch with both ribbing (on
smaller needles) and main stitch pattern. Count your gauge with the knitting
slightly stretched, as it will be when worn.

A = wrist to thumb division
B = wrist to finger division
C, D, E, F = length of 1st,
2nd, 3rd, and 4th fingers
G = length of thumb

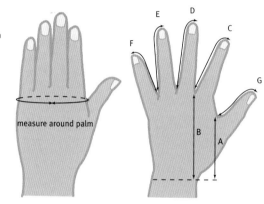

measure around palm

261
Knitting a glove

1 | Knit a glove with fingers in the same way
as a mitten to the base of the fingers; now
thread the stitches onto contrasting yarn.

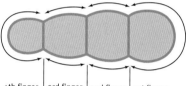

4th finger | 3rd finger | 2nd finger | 1st finger

260
Knitting a mitten

1 | For a standard mitten begin at the
cuff. After knitting the cuff, increase
stitches over the next several rounds to
shape the base of the thumb. The extra
thumb stitches are then slipped onto a
holder, and the remainder of the mitten
completed, decreasing at each side over
the last few rounds to shape the top
of the fingers. At the top, stitches are
arranged on two needles, to be grafted
together (page 146).

2 | Pick up the thumb stitches and
work as a little tube, decreasing at the
top and finally gathering the remaining
stitches together with the tail of the
yarn. This child's mitten features a bold
cable panel on the back of the hand.

2 | Make sure the number of stitches
is accurate for the each finger to be the
correct size. Often little bridges are made
between the fingers by casting on a
couple of stitches.

3 | Beginning with the index finger, pick up
stitches from the contrasting yarn, casting
on for a bridge if required, and work each
finger as a little tube in the same way as
for the mitten thumb (left). Each finger is
finished in turn. For this fingerless glove,
just a few rounds are worked for each finger.

Socks

The most comfortable socks have no seams, being knitted as seamless tubes. It is usual to begin at the top of the sock, then use short-row shaping (page 86) to bend the tube to form a heel, and end by tapering toward the toe. (Socks may also be knitted from the toe upward.)

Leg length: begin below the knee or above the ankle, or allow for a fold-over top as shown here. Use an elastic cast-on edge for a neat fit that will stretch over the foot. Knee-length socks need to be decreased from the top edge down to the ankle, usually at center back of leg.

262

The perfect sock

Toe shaping: this toe is decreased with two short darts (one at each side), and finished by arranging the remaining stitches on two needles and grafting them together (page 146) to avoid a lumpy seam.

Instep shaping: the circumference usually decreases slightly between the heel and the toe.

Heel shaping: there are several ways to shape sock heels using various forms of short-row shaping (page 86), sometimes combined with picking up stitches (page 62). One method is shown below.

263

Working a simple sock heel

1 ❙ Leave half of the stitches on a holder or a spare needle. Work a series of short rows back and forth on the remaining stitches, on two needles, gradually decreasing the number of stitches down to the back of the heel.

2 ❙ Work more short rows to gradually increase the number of stitches in work back to the original number, forming a pouch shape to fit the heel. To avoid making holes at the ends of the short rows, use the wrapped stitch technique (page 86). Then continue knitting the foot and toe.

CREATIVE TECHNIQUES

Unlock your creativity by learning how to dye your own yarns, make felted bags or pillows, knit designs with several colors, work embroidery, knit-in beads, and make knit and crochet trimmings to embellish your work in any way you wish.

Hand-dyeing

There are many types of household and specialist dyes available from drugstores, specialist shops, or via the Internet. Different types of dyes suit different yarn fibers. Most natural fibers dye well, but synthetic yarns are more difficult to dye successfully and some natural-fiber yarns that are pre-treated (e.g. non-shrink) may also be problematic.

264 Hand-dyeing methods

The easiest method of dyeing is to immerse your skein(s) in a dye bath made using dye suitable for the fibers in your yarn. Choose a type of dye to suit your yarn from the table below. Refer to the hand-dyeing checklist below and follow the instructions that come with the dye. Most dyes come in powder form, and you can mix them together if you can't find the shade you want. For more exciting effects, try dip dyeing or rainbow dyeing. Use this chart to select a suitable dye for your yarn.

Type of dye	additives/pre-treatments required	wool and other animal-fiber yarns	cotton, linen, and other plant-fiber yarns	silk yarns	viscose yarns
Cold-water household dye	salt plus brand-name fix or soda ash (sodium carbonate)	no	yes	yes: pale results	yes: pale results
Hot-water household dye	salt plus vinegar / citric acid	yes	no	no	no
Procion dye	salt plus vinegar / citric acid	yes	no	yes	no
Procion dye	salt plus brand-name fix or soda ash (sodium carbonate)	no	yes	yes	yes
Koolaid	none (contains citric acid)	yes	no	yes	yes

265 Hand-dyeing checklist

- For bright, clear colors start with white or natural-colored yarn.
- Prepare the yarn by winding it into a skein (see opposite).
- Weigh the yarn to calculate amounts of dye and additives required according to the instructions supplied with the dye.
- Collect the equipment together: plastic bowls or buckets, stirring sticks or spoons, a measuring jug and, for hot dyeing, heatproof metal or enamel containers (plastic containers for microwave methods). Keep this dyeing equipment separate from kitchen utensils.
- Protect surfaces with plastic sheet or layers of newspaper—dye solutions stain. Wear rubber gloves and an apron.
- Wash and rinse the skeins keeping them wet. Treat with additive if required.
- Follow the instructions supplied with the dye, but bear in mind that skeined yarn is easily damaged. If necessary, gently agitate the dye bath, not the skeins, to prevent rubbing and tangling.
- If you are using a hot-water method, avoid sudden changes of temperature (especially when dyeing woolen yarns), which may felt or shrink the yarn. Heat the dye bath very gently to the required temperature. After dyeing, allow to cool and then rinse with water at the same temperature.
- After rinsing as instructed, do not wring or spin dry; roll the skeins in an old towel to blot away excess moisture. Do not tumble dry.
- Dry the skeins in a warm place away from direct heat and sunlight.
- Use tie-on labels to identify different yarns, dyes, and dyeing methods.

266
Winding yarn into a skein

Skein the yarn by wrapping it around a large piece of cardboard. To prevent tangling, use lengths of spare yarn to tie the skein loosely in several places with a figure eight, then slip the skein off the cardboard.

268
Kool-Aid® dyeing

The samples shown here were dyed with orange Kool-Aid® top is a pure wool yarn, in the center is mohair, and below is a mohair/silk blend; the white ties, which haven't absorbed any color, are cotton.

Kool-Aid® is a soft drink concentrate that is easy and safe to use for home dyeing, but it will only dye animal fibers such as wool or silk. No additives are required because it already contains citric acid. Several different flavors are available, each giving a different color. One 0.14oz (3.9gm) packet will dye about 1oz (28gm) of wool to a medium shade. You will need a plastic container with a lid, large enough to hold the yarn when covered with liquid. To dye your yarn, follow the hand-dyeing checklist until the yarn is wet.

• Tip the Kool-Aid® powder into a plastic container and add enough warm water to cover the yarn. Stir to dissolve.
• Squeeze excess water from the skein and put it in the dye bath, making sure all the yarn is covered.
• Put the lid on loosely and microwave at full power for one minute. Repeat 3 or 4 times until the liquid is nearly boiling. (Time will depend on the power of the microwave). Do not let the liquid dry up. Allow to cool and then rinse in warm water.
• Blot off the excess water in an old towel and dry in a warm place away from direct heat or sunlight.

267
Over-dyeing

The original color of the yarn affects the final color after dyeing. If the yarn is not white, the final color will be a blend of the dye color and the yarn color.

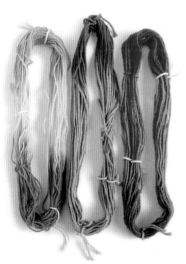

Left to right: pale yellow dip-dyed with green (making sharp green) and blue (making turquoise); pale blue yarn dip-dyed with orange (making brown) and yellow (making green); pink yarn dip-dyed with orange (making sharp red) and blue (making purple).

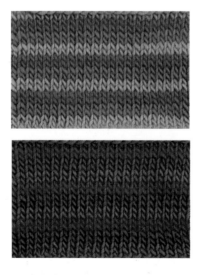

You can over-dye a finished piece of knitting to soften contrasting colors. However, always try a test piece first because the dyeing process may shrink the work.

FIX IT

269 *No microwave?*

Use a metal or enamel container (not aluminum) and simmer on the stove top for 20 minutes or as instructed. Or bake in the oven in any ovenproof container for 20–30 minutes at 275°F / 140°C, or wrap with plastic food wrap and steam in a steamer for 20 minutes (5 minutes in a micro-steamer).

270

Dip dyeing

You will need a stick to hold the skein suspended in the dye bath.

Dip-dyeing a skein of yarn

To dip-dye, follow the manufacturer's instructions to mix the dye with water and make a dye bath. Add fix as instructed. Afterward, rinse and dry the yarn.

Loop the wet, prepared skein over a stick and dip it into the dye bath for the required time. You can gradually raise the height of the stick to shade the yarn from light to dark.

Procion dye is a reliable dye for natural fibers—wool, silk, cotton, and linen. There are many colors available and you can mix dye powder to make many more hues. Colors are strong, permanent, and washable. The samples here were dip-dyed in Procion dye. From left to right they are: mohair, cotton, wool, and silk yarns.

Alternatively, arrange a skein over two dye baths. If left to soak for a time, the white area in the middle will blot up dye and blend the two colors together. Lift out the skeins with a stick.

Three of the test yarns dip-dyed in Procion dye were knitted up into these samples.

271 Rainbow dyeing

You can paint or splash dye onto skeins of yarn. This process works best with Procion dyes, but you can also try cold-water dye, mixed to a strong solution. You will need plastic food wrap and a brush (or a nozzle bottle) for each dye color.

◎**TRY IT**

272 **Natural dyes**

Nettles (green/yellow), madder (rose red), indigo, and other plants are sources of natural dyes giving soft, glowing colors. Most natural dyes require pre-treating (called "mordanting") with various solutions such as alum, cream of tartar, or citric acid, and the processes can be lengthy and complicated. Follow recipes supplied with products exactly.

Rainbow-dyeing a skein

Mix up two or three strong dye solutions and use brushes or nozzle bottles to apply the dyes to the wet, prepared skein. Wrap skeins separately in plastic food wrap to keep them wet for the required amount of time and to prevent colors bleeding from one skein to another. Refer to the hand-dyeing checklist to dry the yarn.

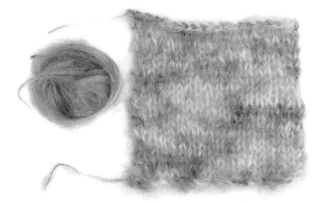

When rainbow-dyed yarns are knitted up, the colors are spotted at random across the work, as shown here.

Felting

When woolen knits are vigorously washed in hot water and then plunged into cold rinsing water, the woolen fibers mat together and the knitting shrinks, forming a sturdy, dense fabric suitable for purses and pillows.

273 Choosing yarn

100% wool yarn works best for felting. Loosely spun wool yarns produce felt with a fuzzy surface in which the individual stitches may be almost indistinguishable. Yarns that are more tightly spun will retain more of the appearance of the individual stitches. Avoid yarns labeled as "machine-washable;" even though they may be 100% wool, they have been specially treated to make them shrink-resistant.

This purse was knitted in stripes of worsted-weight wool using a slipstitch pattern at each color change. The top edge and handle are in garter stitch, finished with a crochet edge. As a rule, assemble a project such as a purse, before felting it and run in all the yarn tails. Use the flat seam method (page 142) to avoid thick, lumpy seams.

274 Making a test piece

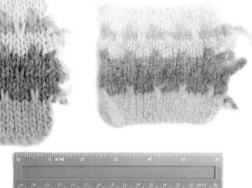

1 | Make a gauge swatch, using your chosen yarns and stitch pattern. Make a note of the numbers of stitches and rows, and the dimensions of the swatch. Wash the swatch in the washing machine with a normal amount of detergent—you can use a half-capacity wash program. Include a large, clean towel or a pair of old jeans to add friction to the wash. Dry the swatch flat.

2 | Measure the swatch to calculate the gauge after felting. Your swatch may shrink by as much as 25% in each direction. The colors may be affected too: they usually fade a little, and blend together in the fuzzy surface of the felt. Now you can use the new gauge to plan a project such as a felted purse or pillow.

FIX IT

275 Want a precise size?

You can shrink a garment, such as a hat, to the exact size you want. Find a bowl or pot of the required circumference and felt the hat by one of the methods described. Leave it stretched over the bowl or cooking pan until it is completely dry.

With a long strap and striking cable-effect front, this felted shoulder bag, designed by Sarah Hatton for Rowan, is both pretty and practical.

276
Adding motifs using a needle-felting kit

As you punch with the tool, five barbed needles (protected by a safety cover) interlace the wool fibers so the design is permanently fixed in place. Woolen yarns give the best results, punched onto a background of felted knitting, as shown. Follow the instructions supplied with the kit.

⟳ TRY IT

Moderate the shrinkage

277 The amount of shrinkage and felting can be controlled by less drastic treatments. Here are two methods:
• Use an old-fashioned top-loading washing machine for the felting. Stop the wash every couple of minutes and lift the knitting out with tongs to check how far it has shrunk. When it has shrunk the required amount, rinse well in cool water and leave flat on a towel to dry.
• Prepare two bowls: one of hot, soapy water (about 85°F or 30°C), and the other of very cold water. You will also need something to rub the knitting on, such as a washboard, and a nailbrush. Wear rubber gloves. Wash the knitting in the hot water for a couple of minutes, then lift it out and rub it vigorously on the washboard until it begins to shrink. Brush the surface gently to fluff up the fibers. Plunge the knitting into the cold water. Repeat the hot/rub/cold process several times if required. Rinse twice more in fresh, cold water, squeeze out excess moisture and leave flat to dry.

Embroider it

278 Felted knitting makes a great surface for freestyle embroidery (page 128) because it is firm and non-elastic: it won't stretch and thereby loosen the embroidery stitches. Use a sharp-pointed needle such as a darning needle to work the embroidery.

Combining yarns for texture

Combine yarns of different textures to transform any project: contrast smooth cottons with fuzzy wools, fluffy mohairs, or sparkling metallics. Whether you want to work simple stripes (page 53), two-color designs (page 122), or an intarsia design (page 124), you can use as many different yarn types as you like, provided they knit to the same gauge.

279 Matching yarn weights

The easiest way to ensure yarn weights are the same is to check the ball band for the same needle size and then knit small swatches to confirm the gauge. Block or press the pieces (page 148) before making a comparison.

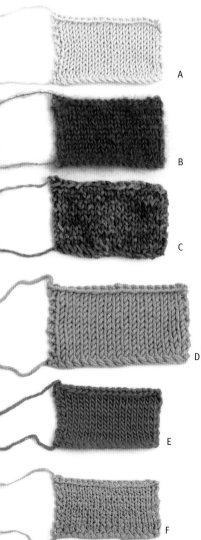

All these yarns are described as worsted or Aran weight. The swatches are all 18 stitches x 12 rows, made on US 8 (5mm) needles. The pale green cotton (A), dark green mohair (B), and green/blue shaded chenille (C) all match in size, so they knit to the same gauge and could be used together in one project. The olive green wool (D) is a little larger and also too firm (this yarn would suit a larger needle size) so this yarn cannot be successfully combined with those above. The turquoise wool swatch (E) is a little too small, but by winding this yarn together with another, finer yarn, the weight (and therefore the gauge) can be increased as necessary. The light turquoise tape swatch (F) is smallest of all. This yarn requires winding together with another medium-weight yarn to achieve the correct gauge.

280 Winding yarns together

If a yarn is too fine for your purpose, you can wind it double or wind it together with another yarn to add extra bulk.

Winding by hand

Wind two yarns together into a small ball and make another swatch. If contrasting colors are used, the effect when knitted will be randomly speckled. Here, the turquoise wool (E) has been wound together with a fine kid mohair yarn to add bulk and color interest. The size and gauge now match the swatches at left.

281 Approximate weight combinations

Yarn weights achieved by combining strands of different yarns:

Combine	to make
2 strands fingering/4-ply	Sport/double knitting weight
1 strand fingering/4-ply + 1 strand sport/double knitting	Worsted/Aran weight
2 strands sport/double knitting	Heavy-weight worsted/Aran
1 strand worsted/Aran + 1 strand fingering/4-ply	Heavy-weight worsted/Aran
1 strand worsted/Aran + 1 strand sport/double knitting	Bulky/chunky
2 strands worsted/Aran	Extra bulky/extra chunky

Using a yarn twister

For speed and consistency, you can twist yarns together using a yarn twister, like the one shown. Here, light turquoise tape (F) has been twisted together with a 4-ply slub cotton of a similar color, making a swatch the same size as those opposite.

This machine winds two strands around each other, so that when the resulting yarn is knitted, the colors are more evenly mixed than if you had wound them by hand. Electric twisters are also available.

282 Improvise a yarn twister

With a little ingenuity, you can improvise a yarn-twisting device with household articles. The two yarns must be arranged one below the other, bringing the lower yarn up through the center of the upper one. Here, the upper yarn (green) is wound around a plastic funnel, which fits over a bowl holding a center-pull ball of the lower yarn (blue). The strand of blue yarn passes up through the funnel, so that as the yarns are wound together into a ball, the green yarn spirals around the blue. Both yarns must flow completely freely as you wind them.

This sideways-knitted vest was made from a very straightforward pattern (originally in stockinette stitch with a crocheted edging), substituting random stripes of differently textured yarns. By introducing textured stitches such as reversed stockinette stitch, slip stitches, and eyelet holes, the regularity of the stripes is broken, adding to the random effect.

🌀TRY IT

283 Use similar colors

For vibrant colors, combine two close shades. Here, two shades of green wool are wound together, knitting up as a speckled tweedy green with depth and richness.

FIX IT

284 *Smooth, slippery yarns knit with uneven stitches?*

Try combining smooth yarns with woolly or fluffy ones such as soft-spun wool or fine kid mohair.

285 *Colors don't blend together?*

Soften the effect of brightly colored stripes by winding each color together with the same fine yarn or thread. The fine multi-colored yarn used here is sold on cones for machine knitting.

Slip-stitch patterns

Versatile slip stitches may be used in many ways to form allover textured stitch patterns. By slipping stitches across color changes, interesting color patterns can be made without knitting with more than one color in a row.

286
Linen stitch

This simple stitch makes a firm, flat fabric that will not curl, with an unusual woven appearance. Requires an odd number of stitches, plus 2 for a selvage stitch at each edge.

Row 1: * K1, yf, sl1p, yb, * repeat from
* to * to the last stitch, K1.
Row 2: P1, * P1, yb, sl1p, yf, * repeat
from * to * to the last 2 stitches, P2.
Repeat these 2 rows.

287
Slip-stitch stripes

Transform simple stripes with regularly placed slip stitches. Requires a multiple of 4 stitches plus 3.

Row 1: Using color A, K.
Row 2: Using color A, P.
Row 3: Change to color B. K3,
* sl1p, K3, * repeat from * to *
to end.
Row 4: P3, * sl1p, P3, * repeat
from * to * to end.
Row 5: as row 3.
Row 6: P.

Row 7: Change to color A. K1, *
sl1p, K3, * repeat from * to * to
last 2 stitches, sl1p, K1.
Row 8: P1, * sl1p, P3, * repeat
from * to * to last 2 stitches,
sl1p, P1.
Row 9: as row 7.
Row 10: P.
Repeat rows 2–10.

288
Broken vertical stripes

This stitch uses the technique of winding the yarn twice (shown at right) to make the slipped stitches looser. Requires a multiple of 4 stitches plus 3.

Row 1: Using color A, K.
Row 2: Using color A, * P3,
P1wtw, * repeat from * to * to
last 3 stitches, P3.
Row 3: Change to color B. * K3,
sl1p del, * repeat from * to * to
last 3 stitches, K3.
Row 4: P1, * P1wtw, P1, sl1p,
P1, * repeat from * to * to last 2
stitches, P1wtw, P1.
Row 5: Change to color A. K1, *
sl1p del, K3, * repeat from * to *

to last 2 stitches, sl1p del, K1.
Row 6: P1, * sl1p, P1, P1wtw,
P1, * repeat from * to * to last 2
stitches, sl1p, P1.
Repeat rows 3–6.
Before binding off or changing to
another stitch pattern, end with
row 3, then work:
Last row: Using color B, P3, *
sl1p, P3, * repeat from * to *
to end.

Purl one, winding yarn twice around needle (P1wtw)

Insert the right-hand needle into the next stitch as if to purl. Wind the yarn twice around the needle and make the purl stitch. This stitch will be slipped on the next row, when the extra loop will be dropped.

Dropping the extra loop (del)

When slipping a stitch made by winding the yarn twice, the extra loop is dropped from the needle, making a long, loose slipped stitch that may be carried up the work (by slipping it on every row) for up to about 4 rows.

289 Mosaic knitting

Mosaic knitting is a technique for working two-color patterns using slip stitches. Stitches are always slipped purlwise (page 57).

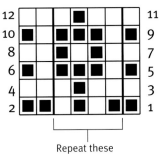

Repeat these 4 stitches

Working mosaic knitting from a chart

Each row of chart squares represents *two* rows of knitting in the same color: a right-side row read from right to left (odd numbers at right of chart), followed by a wrong-side row read from left to right (even numbers at left of chart). On each wrong-side row, the same stitches are slipped as on the previous right-side row.

Alternate rows of chart squares (pairs of rows) are worked in alternate colors—here, rows 1 and 2 in the dark color, rows 3 and 4 in the light color. Each chart row begins with a dark or light square, depending on the color to be used.

Special abbreviations

del = dropping the extra loop (see opposite).
P1wtw = purl one, winding yarn twice around needle (see opposite).
sl1p = slip one purlwise (page 57).
yf = bring the yarn forward between needles, as if to purl.
yb = take the yarn back between needles, as if to knit.

Working the sample pattern

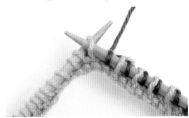

1 | The chart shown requires a multiple of 4 stitches plus 3. Chart row 1 begins at right with a dark square (indicating the dark color for this row), so prepare for mosaic knitting by using the light color to cast on the required stitches. Purl one row. Join in the dark color as on page 52.
Chart row 1 (read right to left): Using the dark color, knit the dark squares and slip the white squares, repeating the 4 stitches as required across the work to the last 2 stitches. That is, K1, * K1, sl1p, * repeat from * to * to last 2 stitches, K2.

2 | **Chart row 2 (read left to right):** Using the dark color, purl the dark squares and slip the white squares (the same stitches as slipped on previous row). That is, P2, * sl1p, P1, * repeat from * to * to last stitch, P1.

3 | **Chart row 3 (read right to left):** Using the light color, knit the white squares and slip the dark squares. That is, K1, * K2, sl1p, K1, * repeat from * to * to last 2 stitches, K2.

4 | **Chart row 4 (read left to right):** Using the light color, purl the white squares and slip the dark squares. That is, P2, * P1, sl1p, P2, * repeat from * to * to the last stitch, P1.

5 | Continue reading from the chart, repeating the 12 chart rows as required.

⊛TRY IT

290 Denser option

For a different texture, work all the wrong-side rows of mosaic knitting as knit instead of purl. This makes a denser, more nubbly fabric. To work the slip stitches on the wrong side rows, yf, slip required stitch(es), yb.

Fair Isle knitting

Fair Isle knitting uses small repeating patterns formed by working two colors in turn along each row. The design can use multiple colors overall, but only two are used at any one time. Two-color knitting is usually worked in stockinette stitch, often using needles one size larger than recommended for plain stockinette stitch.

291
Working with two colors

Fair Isle patterns are usually worked from charts. Soft, elastic yarns such as loosely-spun wool usually work best for this type of work, and after blocking, the two colors should "sit together," making a flat surface with even stitches.

Depending on the size of the pattern, the two colors of any one row can be carried along the row by stranding, weaving, or twisting the color not in use on the wrong side of the work.

292
Stranding

Use this technique to work small repeating patterns. The color not in use is carried loosely across the wrong side of the work, behind no more than 4 stitches. The loose strands so formed are called "floats." For a neat appearance on the right side, one color should always be "below," and the other color, "above," all across each row. Working from the chart above, color A (dark blue) is "below," and color B (light turquoise), "above."

Working from a color chart

Chart rows are numbered from bottom to top, i.e., in the order in which they are worked. Right-side rows (odd numbers) are numbered on the right and read from right to left. Wrong-side rows (even numbers) are numbered on the left and are read from left to right unless you are working circular knitting. There may be one or more edge stitches at one or both sides of the repeating section of the chart. The chart shown requires a multiple of 8 stitches plus 1. The extra stitch at left is worked only once, at the end of each right-side row and the beginning of each wrong-side row.

Chart row 1 (read right to left): Knit * 1A, 2B, 3A, 2B, * repeat from * to * to the last stitch, K1A.

Chart row 2 (read left to right): Purl 1B, * 1A, 2B, 1A, 2B, 1A, 1B, * repeat from * to * to end.

Continue in this way, reading from successive chart rows.

Repeat the 8 chart rows as required.

Repeat these 8 stitches

Work this stitch once

■ = A dark blue

■ = B light turquoise

Stranding on a right-side (K) row

1 ▊ To change from A to B, drop A and bring B over A to knit the required stitches in B. Keep the previous stitches in A well spread out along the right needle so the strand of B is not too tight.

2 ▊ To change from B to A, drop B and bring A under B to knit the stitches in A.

Stranding on a wrong-side (P) row

1 ▊ At the beginning of every row, twist the colors around each other to prevent loose edge stitches. To change from A to B, drop A and bring B over A to purl the stitches in B.

2 ▊ To change from B to A, drop B and bring A under B to purl the stitches in A. On the wrong side, the floats are neatly arranged "above" and "below," without twisting.

293

Weaving

Where a color passes behind more than four stitches, it should be woven over and under one or more of those stitches to prevent long, loose floats that can catch on fingers and jewelry. The weaving can be worked on every second or third stitch to form short floats, or on every stitch to make a firm, solid fabric.

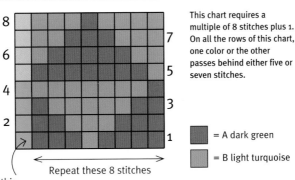

8
7
6
5
4
3
2
1

Work this stitch once

← Repeat these 8 stitches →

This chart requires a multiple of 8 stitches plus 1. On all the rows of this chart, one color or the other passes behind either five or seven stitches.

■ = A dark green

□ = B light turquoise

This baby sweater has a circular-knit yoke with bands of two-color patterning. In circular knitting, the right side of the work is always facing you (page 106).

Weaving on a right-side (K) row

1 To weave B behind a stitch in A bring B over A and then knit one stitch with A.

2 Next bring A under B and continue knitting with A. The strand of B is carried over and then under A.

Weaving on a wrong-side (P) row

1 Bring B over the right needle and purl one stitch with A.

2 Next bring B down, over A, and continue purling with A.

294

Twisting

Twisting can be used as an alternative to weaving. The yarns on the back of the work should be twisted every two or three stitches.

Twisting on a right-side (K) row

Bring A around B from behind and continue knitting with A.

Twisting on a wrong-side (P) row

Bring A around B from below and continue purling with A. At the end of each row, you need to stop and untangle the two colors.

FIX IT

295 *Untidy stitches at the sides?*

Add a single garter-stitch selvage (page 60) at each side and work these extra stitches in the main color, twisting the two colors as left before the last stitch of every row (unless the previous stitch is a contrast color, when this is unnecessary).

296 *Weaving or twisting visible on the right side?*

Sometimes the color carried across the back shows through on the front of the work, especially if the colors used are strongly contrasting. Staggering the position of the woven stitches or twists from one row to the next will help to avoid this.

Intarsia

Intarsia is another name for picture knitting. A charted design is knitted in stockinette stitch using a separate ball of yarn for each area of color. Large single motifs may be knitted or all-over pictorial designs, and small details may be added later with duplicate stitch or other embroidery stitches (pages 126–129).

297
Choosing and preparing yarns

For intarsia patterns, soft, woolly yarns form a more even surface than firm, rounded yarns (such as cotton), which tend to produce uneven stitches.

Count how many separate balls of each color will be required. The flower motif shown right needs two small balls of orange and one very small ball of yellow plus two balls of the main color (green), one for each side of the motif.

For a small design you will only need short lengths of yarn. Wind enough yarn for each color onto small center-pull balls (page 42) or bobbins. To find out how much yarn you need in each color, see the tip below.

299
Calculating yarn quantities

To estimate the amount of yarn needed for an area of color, count the number of chart squares in that color. Wind the yarn around the knitting needle ten times then unwind it and measure the length. This length will knit about ten stitches, so you can calculate the length the area will require. Add 10–20% extra, to be sure.

298
Working from charts

Chart rows are numbered from bottom to top, i.e., in the order in which they are worked. Right-side rows (odd numbers) are numbered on the right, and read from right to left. Wrong-side rows (even numbers) are numbered on the left, and read from left to right. This chart is 19 stitches wide and 26 rows high. Notice how the chart grid is not square but rectangular. This approximates to the average gauge of stockinette stitch. Depending on the design, a whole garment piece may be charted; otherwise, pattern instructions will tell you where to place the charted stitches within the knitting, as shown below.

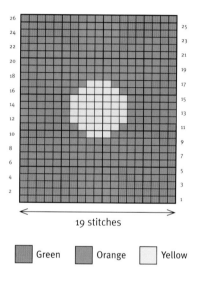

19 stitches

■ Green   ■ Orange   □ Yellow

Working from the sample chart

1 ❙ Work to the length required before the charted area begins. On the next row (normally a right-side row), knit to the edge of the charted area and place a marker on the right-hand needle. Chart row 1 reads: K8 green, 3 orange, 8 green. So, knit the next 8 stitches in green. To join in the orange, insert the right needle into the next stitch in the usual way and hold a 6in (15cm) tail to the left. Wrap the yarn counter-clockwise around the right needle and flip the tail across the working yarn. This little twist helps to keep the first stitch tighter.

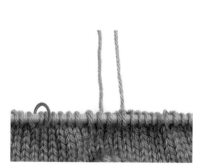

2 ❙ Pull the new loop through to make the stitch and then knit the rest of the stitches required in this color. Join in new balls as needed and complete the first row of chart stitches. Place a ring marker on the needle and complete the row.

3 | On the next row, purl to the first marker, slip it, then count the stitches from the chart. To change from one color to the next, drop the first color, then bring the new color up behind the first. Crossing the yarns in this way prevents holes in the work. Work the first stitch in the new color tightly. Complete the chart stitches, changing colors as necessary. Slip the second marker and complete the row.

4 | On the following row, knit to the first marker and slip it, then work the charted stitches. To change from one color to the next, drop the first color and bring the new color up behind it, crossing the colors at the wrong side of the work. Knit the first stitch in the new color tightly. Complete the chart stitches, changing colors as necessary. Slip the second marker and complete the row.

5 | Continue to work the design in the same way. As a general rule, avoid making floats (they can pull the knitting out of shape). However, sometimes it makes sense to have them, as on rows 4 and 5 of the flower chart. Floats may be stranded, darned, or twisted as for Fair Isle knitting (pages 122–123).

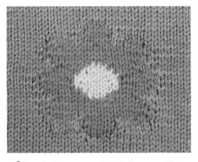

6 | When the knitted piece is complete, don't worry if the stitches look uneven. Finishing off the tails correctly will improve the appearance. On the wrong side, pull gently on all the tails to tighten any loose stitches. Thread each tail in turn into a tapestry needle and darn it in and out of the loops along the edge of an area of color for 1–2in (2.5–5cm). Snip off the excess.

7 | Carefully press or block (page 148) the piece. If you are making a garment, this should be done once all the knitting has been completed but before assembly.

FIX IT

300 *Uneven stitches?*
Stitches next to color changes often look uneven, with a tight stitch on one row and a loose stitch on the next. Use a tapestry needle to gently ease the tight stitches, pulling excess yarn through from the loose stitch above or below.

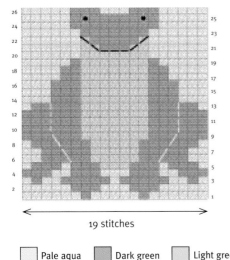

19 stitches

This frog motif is embellished with embroidery. Backstitch is used in the background color to outline the legs, and in black for the mouth. The eyes are made with black French knots surrounded by orange single chain stitches (page 128).

☐ Pale aqua ■ Dark green ☐ Light green

Counted-stitch embroidery

This type of embroidery is usually worked from a chart onto knitting worked in stockinette stitch. There are two different counted stitches you can use: duplicate stitch (sometimes called Swiss darning), and cross stitch. Both are best used for outline designs because if they are used to fill large areas, the knitting becomes solid and inflexible. (If you want to work a design with large areas of solid color, use the intarsia technique on page 124.) It is often easier to work embroidery before assembling a garment or other project.

301 Counted stitch embroidery guidelines

- Always use a blunt-tipped tapestry needle to avoid splitting the knitted stitches.
- Choose yarn for embroidery of the same fiber as the knitting.
- Cut lengths of embroidery yarn no longer than 24 in (60cm).
- Decide where the center of the chart will be positioned on the knitting.
- Begin by passing the needle through to the back of the work, leaving a 4 in (10cm) tail on the surface to be run in later.
- Begin stitching at or near the center of the design and work outward.
- Do not pull stitches too tightly.
- Don't pass the embroidery yarn behind more than three stitches between embroidered areas—fasten off and start again.
- When complete, run in all the tails along the back of matching embroidery stitches, where they will not show.

This design may be embroidered in either duplicate stitch (below) or cross stitch (opposite). Note that the chart is drawn on a non-square grid, corresponding to the average knitted gauge of stockinette stitch, with more rows to 4in (10cm) than there are stitches to 4in (10cm).

302 Duplicate stitch

Each square on the chart represents one knitted stitch and each duplicate stitch exactly covers one knitted stitch. The embroidery yarn follows the path of the knitted yarn. Choose a contrasting yarn of a similar weight to that used for the knitting, or slightly heavier for good coverage.

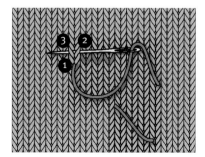

1 Insert the needle about 2in (5cm) away from where you intend to start the embroidery. Bring the needle out at 1, the base of the knitted stitch you want to duplicate. Pull up the yarn, leaving a 4in (10cm) tail of yarn on the surface (this will be run in later). Pass the needle behind the two "legs" of the stitch above, from 2 to 3. Pull through.

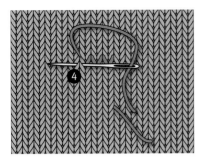

2 | Insert the needle again at 1, and bring it out at 4, the base of the next knitted stitch to be duplicated. Here, a line of duplicate stitch is being worked from right to left, so you can pass the needle from 1 to 4 in one movement. Repeat as required, counting the stitches carefully.

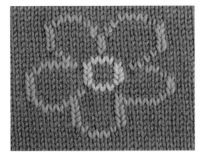

Try to match the embroidery to the size of the knitted stitches by using a yarn of the same weight or even slightly heavier.

305 Cross stitch

Each colored square on the chart represents one cross stitch. However, each chart square does not correspond to a knitted stitch—instead, each intersection of the grid lines represents the center of a knitted stitch. Choose a lighter-weight contrasting yarn.

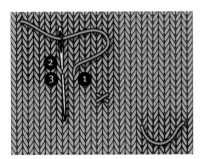

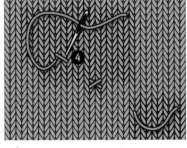

1 | Insert the needle about 2in (5cm) away from where you intend to start the embroidery. Bring the needle out at 1, the bottom-right corner of the first cross stitch, at the center of a knitted stitch, leaving a tail on the surface as for duplicate stitch. Insert the needle at 2, the top-left corner of the cross stitch, at the center of the knitted stitch. Bring it out again at 3, one knitted stitch below 2.

2 | Pull through gently and insert the needle at 4, at the top-right corner of the cross stitch, again at the center of a knitted stitch. Pull through gently. Repeat as required, counting the stitches carefully.

For an even appearance, make sure that all the top threads of the crosses all slope in the same direction.

TRY IT

306 Add details

Use duplicate stitch to add small details (such as eyes, noses, or flower centers) to intarsia motifs, avoiding the need for many small balls of yarn in work.

Embellish textured or lace knitting with motifs worked in cross or duplicate stitch, as in the samples shown here.

A child's sweater embroidered with a cross stitched cat (taken from the child's own drawing). French knots (page 129) in green are used for the eyes.

Freestyle embroidery

Many freestyle embroidery stitches can be used to decorate knitwear worked in stockinette stitch; some of the most useful are described below. As a rule, avoid heavy, close embroidery stitches, which will tend to distort the knitting. You can place an embroidered detail anywhere you like to make your project special.

307 Freestyle embroidery guidelines

• Use a sharp needle with a large eye, such as a darning needle.
• Choose smooth yarn for embroidery of the same fiber as the knitting, and of a similar weight or a little lighter.
• Cut lengths of embroidery yarn no longer than 24 in (60cm).
• Begin by passing the needle through to the back of the work, leaving a 4 in (10cm) tail on the surface to be run in later.
• Do not pull stitches too tightly or the knitting will be distorted.
• Don't pass the embroidery yarn behind more than two or three stitches between embroidered areas—fasten off and start again.
• When complete, run in all the tails along the back of matching embroidery stitches where they will not show.

308 Chain stitch

Use a continuous line of chain stitch for straight or curved lines and outlines. Bring the needle up at 1, form a loop with the thread and insert the needle again at 1. Bring it up at 2, inside the loop of thread, and pull through. Now make another loop, insert the needle again at 2 and bring it out at 3. Repeat as required, ending with a little stitch to hold the last loop in place.

309 Single chain stitch

Sometimes called Lazy Daisy Stitch, this stitch is often used for flower petals and little leaves.

Bring the needle up at 1, form a loop with the thread and insert the needle again at 1. Bring the needle up again at 2, inside the loop. Pull through gently. Now insert the needle at 3, catching down the loop of thread. By moving point 3 a short distance further away from point 2, a little tail will be formed.

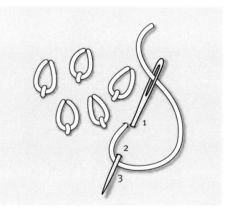

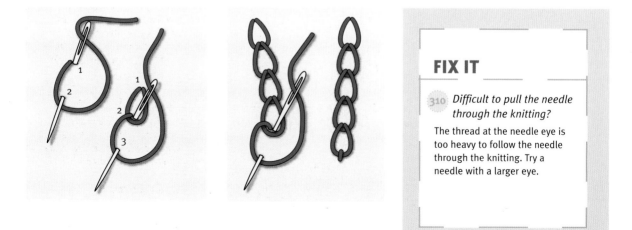

FIX IT

310 *Difficult to pull the needle through the knitting?*

The thread at the needle eye is too heavy to follow the needle through the knitting. Try a needle with a larger eye.

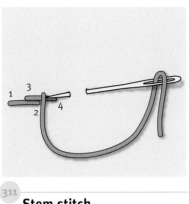

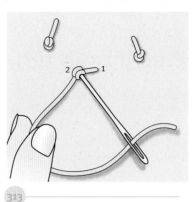

311 Stem stitch

Stem stitch makes a more slender line than chain stitch.

Work the line from left to right. Bring the needle up at 1 and insert it at 2, then bring it out at 3, (midway between 1 and 2), and above the thread. Pull through. Insert the needle next at 4 and then bring it out again above the previous stitch and halfway along it. Pull through. Repeat to the right.

312 French knots

Use these little knots for flower centers, animal eyes, or other small details.

Bring the needle up at 1 and wind the thread twice around the needle tip. Holding the thread, insert the needle very close to—but not exactly at—1 and pull through gently.

313 Knots with tails

For a French knot with a little tail, insert the needle at 2, a short distance away from 1 and pull through. The knot will form at 2. Isolated French knots may be finished by tying the two thread tails with a square knot on the wrong side, and snipping to leave tails of about ½in (12mm).

314 Placing embroidery

1 | Use a water-erasable marking pen to trace the design onto lightweight, non-fusible interfacing (or tissue paper). Place the knitting flat and pin the tracing where required, then baste it in place with ordinary sewing thread, avoiding the traced outlines. The basted tracing makes a fairly firm surface, and the knitting will not stretch while you work.

2 | Work the embroidery through both layers and secure all the thread ends on the wrong side. Pull out the basting and then gently tear away the tracing (use tweezers to remove all the shreds).

The embroidery on this child's wrapover top is designed to suit the shape of the right front. It is worked in stem stitch, single chain stitch, and French knots, with and without tails.

⊚TRY IT

315 Use embroidery yarns

If you need just small quantities of yarns for embroidery, consider buying embroidery threads. For woolen knits, choose small skeins of Persian yarn or tapestry yarn: there's a huge range of colors to choose from, and you can combine any number of strands to make the weight of thread you need. Cotton knits may be embroidered with soft embroidery cotton or pearl cotton; cotton floss is too fine for all but the lightest-weight knits.

316 When to embroider

Sometimes it is easier to work the embroidery before the project is assembled, such as on a small purse or a narrow sleeve.

317 Adding sparkle and texture

Sew on beads or sequins to enhance the design.

Knitting with beads and sequins

Although you can work different colors and textures into your knitting with yarn and stitch, it is sometimes fun to add a fresh element. Beads or sequins can look wonderful if they are chosen well and used selectively, perhaps to highlight a motif or create an unusual border design.

318 Choosing beads or sequins

Washability Depending on your project, you may need washable beads or sequins.
Weight The knitted yarn needs to be strong enough to support the beads comfortably, without sagging, so if you are working with a soft yarn avoid beads that are large and heavy.
Hole size Beads to be knitted in should have holes that are large enough to let the bead move easily along the yarn. If you want to use small beads, you'll need to sew them in place. Beads or sequins to be sewn on may have holes of any size.

319 Knitting-in beads or sequins

Before you start to knit the beaded section, calculate how many beads or sequins you need for your design and thread them onto the yarn using a darning needle that fits easily through the holes. You may be able to do this simply by threading the yarn into the darning needle and slipping the needle through each bead in turn. If this proves difficult, try using a leader thread, as explained below. Once all the beads or sequins are on the yarn you can knit them into your work following the instructions, right.

320 Using a leader thread

If the bead holes are too small to take a darning needle threaded with your yarn, use a finer leader thread such as doubled sewing cotton, as shown. However, the bead holes must be large enough to allow the beads to slip easily along the yarn without fraying it.

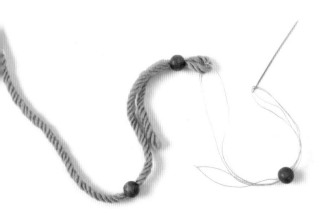

321 Knitting-in beads with a slip stitch

This method is used on a background of stockinette stitch and it is useful because beads can be added on knit or purl rows.

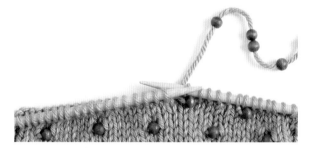

On a right-side (knit) row, work to where the bead is required. Bring the yarn to the front between the needles. Slip the next stitch purlwise, then push a bead along the yarn, up against the right-hand needle. Take the yarn to the back. Knit the next stitch.

On a wrong side (purl) row, purl to where a bead is required. Take the yarn back between the two needles and slip the next stitch purlwise. Push a bead along the yarn so that it sits behind the slipped stitch. Now bring the yarn to the front; purl the next stitch.

On the right side of the knitting each bead sits in front of a slipped stitch.

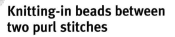

Knitting-in beads between two purl stitches

In this method each bead is held in place by a purl stitch on either side, so the bead sits between two stitches.

Work to one stitch before the required position then purl one; push the bead along the yarn, tight against the right-hand needle and purl one. Complete the row as required.

Knitting-in beads between two knit stitches on a wrong-side row

This method is often used to add beads to garter stitch.

On a wrong-side row, work to one stitch before the required position then knit one; push the bead along the yarn, tight against the right-hand needle, knit one. Complete the row as required.

This purse is decorated with a heart motif of knitted-in beads, worked from a chart. To match the bead colors on the chart, thread the beads in reverse order.

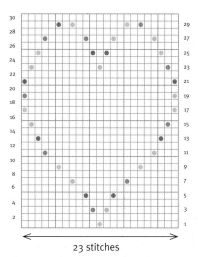

23 stitches

Refer to this chart to knit the beaded heart design shown on the bag, left, using the slip-stitch method, opposite.

On the right side, each bead sits between two purl stitches.

Sewing on beads or sequins

To sew on beads or sequins, use a beading needle (a very slim sewing needle with a small eye), or any sharp sewing needle that fits easily through the beads or sequins.

Sewing on beads

Use thread double and secure it firmly with tiny backstitches behind the bead. Bring the needle through to the right side of the work and thread a bead onto the needle. Take a small stitch through the knitting and pull the thread through. Pass the needle through the bead again, then take the needle through to the wrong side of the work. Make another small backstitch on the wrong side, where it will be hidden by the bead.

Attaching a sequin with a bead

A neat way to attach sequins is to secure each one with a tiny bead at the center. Secure the thread, bring the needle up where required, thread on a sequin and then a small bead. Take the needle back down through the center of the sequin. Repeat the stitch through the bead once more, then secure the thread on the wrong side.

Pompoms, tassels, fringes, and cords

Add the final touch to any project: a pompom or tassel on a hat, a fringe on a scarf, cord ties to fasten a jacket, or cord handles on a purse. It is often the trimmings that can turn an ordinary item into something special that stands out from the crowd.

Pompoms

Add pompoms to hats and scarves, or sew them to the ends of tie fastenings. You can easily make your own from yarn remnants, either using the materials you have at home or with the aid of an inexpensive kit.

325 **Knitted pompom**

This method makes a firm pompom that will not fray. Size depends on yarn and needles used. Use long needles of the recommended size for your yarn.
Cast on 135 stitches.
Knit 1 row.
Dec row: * S2togpo*, repeat from * to * to end.
Repeat the dec row until 5 stitches remain. Cut the yarn, leaving an 8in (20cm) tail.
Thread the tail into a tapestry needle and slip through the remaining 5 stitches. Gather them tightly and secure.
Try changing colors after the first row. Alternatively, omit the bind-off and continue on the last 5 stitches to make a knitted cord as explained on page 135.

326

Making a pompom using cardboard discs
You can make your own winders for pompoms using a pair of compasses and thin cardboard.

1 ❙ Using the compasses, draw two matching circles on cardboard, each with a small circle at the center. Cut out the large and small circles and cut away a wedge. Place the shapes together and wind yarn around them as fully as possible. Use several colors if you wish.

2 ❙ Carefully insert the point of scissors between the cardboard layers and cut all around.

3 ❙ Tie a length of yarn tightly around the center, between the cardboard layers, then pull away the cardboard. Do not trim the tie ends yet—use them to stitch the pompom where required. Snip off any untidy ends.

These pompoms were made using cardboard discs. They are sewn onto crochet ties to create an attractive fastening.

327 Using a pompom maker

Pompom makers are little plastic frames, available in various sizes, with four sections for each size. These have the advantage of being perfectly round and reusable. Follow the manufacturer's instructions.

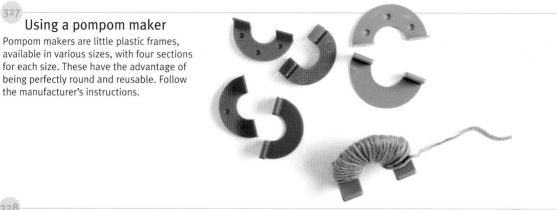

328 Tassels

Trim a hat, a purse, or the corners of a pillow with matching or contrasting tassels.

Making a tassel

There are many ways of making tassels, but the method described here is simple and straightforward.

1 | Cut a piece of firm cardboard to suit the length of tassel you want. Wind yarn around it to the required fullness.

2 | Thread a separate length of yarn into a tapestry needle and slip it under the wrapped yarn at one edge of the cardboard. Tie the ends tightly.

3 | Cut the yarn along the opposite edge of the cardboard. Remove from cardboard and slip the needle down through the top of the tassel, emerging a short distance below.

4 | Bind the yarn tightly around the tassel. Pass the needle under the binding and back to the knot at the top. Use this yarn to attach the tassel, as required.

Two tassels made in different yarns: turquoise mohair and soft green wool.

329

Fringes

Add a fringe to a scarf, purse, or other accessory. Use yarn to match the project, or choose a well-draping yarn such as viscose or silk to add swing to a fringe. You will need a piece of firm cardboard, scissors, and a crochet hook.

1 **I** Cut a piece of cardboard a little wider than the depth of fringe you want. Wind yarn around it and cut along one edge to make lots of identical lengths of yarn.

4 **I** Place the work flat and trim all the ends to exactly the same length.

2 **I** Take two or three lengths and double them. Insert the crochet hook from wrong side to right side, one stitch (or row) in from the edge of the knitting; catch the loop and pull it through the knitting.

3 **I** Catch the strands again and pull them through the loop. Repeat as required.

330

Making a sideways knitted fringe

This fringe has a short knitted border, making it easy to attach to a garment or other item. Use the needle size recommended for your yarn.

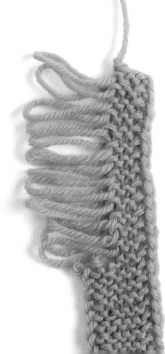

Cast on 7 stitches (or more for a longer fringe). Work in garter stitch (all rows knit) to the length required. The sample shown was worked with a garter-stitch selvage (page 61). To form the fringe, bind off the first 3 stitches, cut the yarn and pull through. Drop the remaining stitches from the needle and unravel them all the way down. Block the fringe (page 148) to remove kinks, allow to dry and sew in place. Cut through all the loops, or leave them uncut, as desired.

331 Twisted, braided, and knitted cords

Cords are useful as drawstrings or ties, or to attach a tassel to an item, such as a hat. They can be twisted, braided or knitted, according to preference.

Making a twisted cord

1 Cut two or more lengths of yarn, each about 3 times the final length required. Knot the ends and secure to a firm surface with masking tape or a pin. Hold the free ends and twist between your fingers until the whole length is very tightly twisted. Don't let go.

2 Hold the center point and bring the two ends together. Release the center and the braid will twist up around itself. Knot all the ends together and run the braid through your fingers to even out the twists.

Here, twisted braids are used to form a fringe. To make this fringe, thread the lengths of yarn through the knitted edge before twisting them. Twist them into cords then trim the knotted ends into little tassels.

332 Making a braided cord

Strands of yarn can be braided (plaited) in the same way as you braid hair. Cut the strands longer than the braid length required because the braiding process will use up extra yarn.

Group strands of yarn into three and braid in the usual way. In the sample at the top, three groups of three strands each form a neat braid, knotted at the end and trimmed into a tassel. In the second sample, each group of strands is a different color, with a bead added to each group below the knot at one end.

333 Making knitted cord (I-cord)

Sometimes called an I-cord (or idiot-cord, because it's so easy), tubular knitted cord is made on two double-pointed needles, two sizes smaller than recommended for your yarn.

Cast on four or five stitches. * Knit 1 row. Do not turn the work. Push the stitches along to the other end of the right needle and hold this needle in your left hand. Bring the yarn tightly across the back of the work. * Repeat from * to * to length required. Bind off. Pulling gently, run the cord through your fingers to even out the stitches.

I-cord is very pliable, and easy to knit. Knit up a short sample first so you can decide how many stitches to work with.

⊚TRY IT

334 I-cord patterns

Lengths of knitted cord can be sewn down to make free-form designs, or to imitate cables.

Flower trims

Turn a plain knit into something special—decorate accessories such as hats, purses, or scarves with these sew-on knitted flowers and leaves. Choose any yarn: wool, cotton, mohair, or lurex. Tape and ribbon yarns give an interesting effect. The thickness of the yarn will determine the size of the flower. As a rule, use the needle size recommended on the yarn ball band. Leave long tails at the beginning and end of each piece, and use these to sew the trims in place.

335 Clematis

Yarn: DK wool in purple (A) and yellow (B)

PETALS (make 6) Using A, cast on 8 sts.
1st row: (RS) K2tog, k4, kfb, k1.
2nd row: K.
Repeat first and 2nd rows 3 times, then work first row again. Bind off knitwise.

CENTER Using B, cast on 12 sts.
1st row: (RS) Make a loop on each st: k1 but do not slip st from needle; bring yarn over between needles, take it clockwise around left thumb and back between needles; k st on left-hand needle again, slipping it off in the usual way; on right-hand needle slip 2nd st over st just made. Bind off, working k2tog across the row.

MAKING UP Leaving the center open, join petals to halfway along inner edges. Pinch a tuck at the inner corner of each petal and stitch. Join ends of center to make a ring and stitch it closed. Set center on petals.

336 Dahlia

Yarn: DK wool

SMALL PETALS Cast on 8 sts.
1st row: (WS) P.
2nd row: K.
3rd row: Bind off 4 sts knitwise, k to end. 4 sts.
4th row: K4, turn, cast on 4 sts by cable method. 8 sts.
Repeat 1st–4th rows 7 times, ending with a 3rd row. 4 sts.
Do not break yarn.

MEDIUM PETALS Next row k4, turn, cast on 6 sts. 10 sts.
*1st row: (WS) P.
2nd row: K.
3rd row: Bind off 6 sts, k to end. 4 sts.
4th row K4, turn, cast on 6 sts. 10 sts. Repeat 1st–4th rows from * 5 times, ending with a 3rd row. 4 sts. Do not break yarn.

LARGE PETALS Next row k4, turn, cast on 8 sts. 12 sts.
** 1st and 3rd rows: P.
2nd and 4th rows: K.
5th row: Bind off 8 sts, k to end. 4 sts.
6th row: K4, turn, cast on 8 sts. 12 sts. Repeat 1st–6th rows from ** 5 times, ending with a 5th row. Do not break yarn.
Work 10 more medium petals, ending with a 3rd row. 4 sts.
Bind off.
MAKING UP Beginning at the cast-on edge and reverse st-st to the outside, coil petals, securing them as you go.

337 Small leaf

Yarn: DK wool

Using 2 double-pointed needles, cast on 3 sts and make a 1¼in (3cm) cord.
Continue on these sts in rows in the usual way:
1st row: (RS) K1, yo, k1, yo, k1. 5 sts.
2nd and WS rows: K.
3rd row: K2, yo, k1, yo, k2. 7 sts.
5th row: K3, yo, k1 yo, k3. 9 sts.
7th row: K4, yo, k1, yo, k4. 11 sts.
9th row: K5, yo, k1, yo, k5. 13 sts.
11th row: Ssk, k9, k2tog. 11 sts.
13th row: Ssk, k7, k2tog. 9 sts.
15th row: Ssk, k5, k2tog. 7 sts.
17th row: Ssk, k3, k2tog. 5 sts.
19th row: Ssk, k1, k2tog. 3 sts.
21st row: Sk2po. Fasten off remaining st.

Specific abbreviation

sk2po—slip one knitwise, k2tog, pass slipped st over.

338 Double daisy

Yarn: DK cotton in white (A), fine cotton in white (B), and yellow (C)

LOWER PETALS Using A, cast on 9 sts by the cable method
1st row: (RS) P.
2nd row: K.
3rd row: Bind off 5 sts purlwise, p2, turn, with yarn at back slip
1 st purlwise, bring yarn to front, p2. 4 sts.
4th rowv K.
5th row: P.
6th row: Kfb, slip these 2 sts on to left-hand needle, cast on
4 sts by cable method, p all 9 sts. Repeat 2nd–6th rows 8 times and then work 2nd and 3rd rows again. 10 petals. Bind off.

UPPER PETALS Using B, work as lower petals.
Center Using C, cast on 5 sts by long-tail cast-on method
1st row: (RS) Kfb, k2, kfb, k1. 7 sts.
2nd and WS rows: K.
3rd row: Kfb, k4, kfb, k1. 9 sts.
4th–10th rows: K.
11th row: K1, k2tog, k3, k2tog, k1. 7 sts.
12th row: [K1, k2tog] twice, k1. 5 sts. Bind off.

MAKING UP Join ends of each strip of petals and lightly gather inner edges of rings, leaving a space in the center. Place upper ring of petals on lower one and stitch together leaving petals free. Padding it slightly with spare yarn, set the center in place and sew on the right side with small running stitches, 1 st in from the edge. Work a few stitches across the space at the back.

A classic clothespin bag, made from a wooden coat hanger and linen tea towels. It features a snap fastening hidden by a lovely knitted cotton daisy, making laundry day a little more special!

⊚TRY IT

339 Add variety

• Vary the size of single petals and leaves by working extra rows of increases and decreases, and/or by working more stockinette rows in the middle.
• Add beads, buttons, sequins, tassels, etc. to flower centers.
• Make a removable decoration by working two or three flowers and attaching them to a brooch pin or safety pin.

Crochet edgings

Crochet edgings are quick to work and help the edges of knitting to lie flat without curling. They can also be used to firm up a loose edge. Here are three simple crochet edgings and the stitches you need to make them.

340

Starting a crochet edging

Like knitting needles, crochet hooks should be chosen to suit your yarn. A hook size may be recommended on the ball band; for edgings, choose one or two sizes smaller. A good tip is to use your gauge sample to try out a few crochet edgings. The edging should lie flat. If it is too tight or too loose, try changing the hook size. For US/metric hook sizes, see page 156.

Starting a crochet edging on a side edge

With the right side of the knitting facing you, work along the knitted edge from right to left. Insert the hook one whole stitch in from a side edge, catch the yarn with the hook and pull through a loop. Leave a tail of at least 4in (10cm) on the wrong side.

Starting on a cast-on or bound-off edge

Leave a tail of at least 4in (10cm) on the wrong side. On a cast-on edge, insert the hook between two stitches of the first row. On a bound-off edge, insert the hook through the center of a stitch.

341

Basic crochet stitches

The three crochet edgings shown opposite can be worked using three basic crochet stitches combined in different ways: chain stitch, slip stitch, and single crochet.

Working chain stitch (ch)

1 | Hold the yarn in your left hand in the same way as for the Continental knitting method (page 46). This stitch always begins with one loop already on the hook. Catch the yarn with the hook.

2 | Pull a new loop through the loop on the hook. You have made a chain stitch.

Working slip stitch (ss)

Insert the hook where instructed (in a previous crochet stitch, or in the edge of the knitting as shown here) and catch the yarn with the hook. Pull a new loop through both the previous work and the loop on the hook. You have made one slip stitch.

Working single crochet (sc)

Insert the hook where instructed, catch the yarn and pull a loop through, making two loops on the hook. Catch the yarn again and pull a new loop through both loops on the hook. You have worked one single crochet stitch.

Working two single crochets together (abbreviation: 2sc tog)

Sometimes you need to decrease by working two single crochet stitches together.

* Insert the hook as instructed, catch the yarn and pull through a loop, * repeat once from * to * in the next position as instructed, making three loops on the hook. Catch the yarn again and pull a new loop through all three loops on the hook. Two single crochet stitches have been worked together, making one new stitch. Three or more sc may be worked together in a similar way.

Simple crochet edgings

Here are three quite different yet simple crochet edgings for you to try. If you are planning to work a crochet edging, add a garter-stitch selvage (page 60) to the side edges of your knitting to make it easy to insert the hook correctly on the first row of the edging.

Making a single crochet edge

Using the same weight of yarn as the knitting and a hook one or two sizes smaller than recommended, begin as opposite, then work 1 ch.

First row: Along a cast-on or bound-off edge, work 1 sc for each knitted stitch; along a side edge, 1 sc in every row may be too many (stretching the edge) so either skip a row at intervals or plan to work 2 sc tog at intervals on the next row.
At outer corners: Work 3 sc in the same place. **At inner corners:** Work 3 sc tog.
At the end of the row: Fasten off with 1 ch, cut yarn and pull through leaving a 4in (10cm) tail. Alternatively, continue with a second row.

Second and following rows: To work another row, work 1 ch, turn the work around and work 1 sc in each sc of the previous row, inserting the hook under both threads at the top of each stitch. Work the corners in the same way as for first row.

Working a picot edge

Picots are made by working little loops of several chain stitches.

Begin by working one or more rows of single crochet. At the end, work 1 ch, turn.
Picot row: Skip the first sc. * 1 sc in next sc, 3 ch, 1 ss in same sc as before, 1 sc in next sc, *. Repeat from * to * to the end. To make the picots larger, work 4 or 5 ch instead of 3 ch.

Working a reversed twist stitch edge

This edging makes a neatly twisted finish.

Begin with one or more rows of single crochet as above. At the end, work 1 ch, but do not turn the work. **Reverse twist row (worked from left to right):** Insert the hook through the next stitch to the right, under two top threads of the stitch. Catch the yarn and pull it through beneath the loop already on the hook. Catch the yarn again and pull it through both loops on the hook. Work 1 ch, skip next sc.* Repeat from * to * to end. (There is usually no need to work extra stitches at outer corners. Skip one or two stitches at inner corners if this improves the appearance.)

This little jacket is bordered with picot edging, worked in rounds instead of rows. Begin the first round of sc at one side seam and end it with 1 ss into first ch of first round. Do not turn the work. Work 1 ch then work the second (picot) round, fastening off with 1 ss into the first ch of the second round. The tie fastenings are made with lengths of chain stitches, finished with pompoms (page 132).

ASSEMBLY

For a truly professional finish, spend time assembling your work with care—slapdash finishing won't do justice to your work. Choose the right seam(s) to suit your project, learn about blocking and pressing, and how to look after your knits so they will last for years in good condition.

Stitching the seams

Hand knitted items are best joined with hand stitching because knitting is stretchy and therefore difficult to sew neatly on a sewing machine. There are several different methods of joining seams, suitable for different yarns, stitches, and purposes.

343

Tips for stitching seams

• When following a commercial pattern using the recommended yarn, use the seaming method and assembly order described in the instructions.
• To assemble a standard sweater, first join the shoulder seams. Next match the top edges of the sleeves to the armholes and

join those. Beginning at the cuffs, join the sleeve seams. Lastly, beginning at the lower edge, join the side seams.
• Use the same yarn as the knitting, or a finer yarn of similar color and fiber content.
• Always use a yarn needle or tapestry needle with a large eye to suit the yarn and a blunt tip to avoid splitting the knitted stitches.
• Use small, sharp scissors to cut yarn.

Ladder stitch seam

Also known as mattress stitch or invisible seam, this seam matches the two edges to be joined, row-for-row, and is almost invisible on the right side of the work. However, it is usually worked one stitch in from each edge, so the finished seam has a certain bulk, making it unsuitable for garments for small babies (for which the flat seam, page 142, is more suitable).

If you work the knitting with a single selvage stitch (page 60) at each edge, as shown below, it will be easier to see where to place the seam stitches. It is not necessary to pin the seam because the edges will be matched row-for-row.

344

Working a ladder-stitch seam on stockinette stitch

1 ❙ At the base of a side or sleeve seam, the two edges should be brought exactly together. If you have left a long cast-on tail, thread it into a yarn needle and hold the two edges side-by-side, with the right side facing. Pass the needle from below, beneath two threads at the base of the first stitch on the opposite edge.

2 ❙ Pull the needle and yarn through. Now pass the needle from below, beneath the corresponding two threads on the first edge, making a figure eight.

Threading a yarn needle
Fold the end of the yarn over the tip of the needle to make a tight loop. Hold the two ends close to the needle. Slide the needle out of the loop. Push the loop through the needle eye.

3 | On the second edge, pass the needle beneath the bar of the first row, between the first and second stitches, one whole stitch in from the edge.

4 | Pull the needle through and pass it beneath two bars (first and second rows) of the first edge.

5 | Repeat the last step on the second and first edges alternately, always inserting the needle where it last emerged and passing it beneath two bars. On this striped knitting, the row ends are seen to match exactly. Notice how the pink seam stitches don't show, even on the stripes of other colors.

345

Working a ladder-stitch seam on other stitches

If your knitting has been worked in reverse stockinette stitch, garter stitch or seed stitch, for example, you'll produce a neater effect by passing the needle beneath just one bar at a time all along the seam, as shown.

346

Ladder stitching a vertical edge to a horizontal edge

Sometimes you need to join a bound-off or cast-on edge to a side edge, as at the top of a sleeve. Pin the seam first using safety pins or large-headed pins, spreading any fullness evenly.

1 | With the right sides of the work facing up, bring the needle up through the center of a stitch on the horizontal edge and then pass it beneath one or two bars of the side edge.

2 | Insert the needle back through the same stitch center on the horizontal edge and bring it up through the next stitch center. Repeat along the edge, making one stitch for every bound-off or cast-on stitch, and taking up one or two bars from the side edge, as necessary, to keep the seam flat.

347 Flat seam

This seam is not quite as neat as a mattress stitch seam, or as strong. Use it for baby garments to avoid bulk, and also for textured yarns that will disguise the seam. Pieces to be joined should be knitted without selvage stitches, unless these are intended as a feature to emphasize the seam.

Working a flat seam

1 Begin at a lower edge with a figure eight, as for ladder stitch (see page 141). Pass the needle through the first edge to the wrong side and hold the work with the wrong side facing. Insert the needle through the knot of the first stitch on the second edge, then through the corresponding knot on the first edge. Repeat along the seam.

2 Tension the stitching so that the yarn holds the edges together snugly. Do not pull too tightly or the seam may pucker the work, or break in use. On the right side the seam should appear as shown here.

348 Backstitch seam

Backstitch makes a strong, firm seam that will not stretch out of shape. Use it to give structure to a garment, for example on shoulder seams, or to take in fullness. The seam should be worked as close to the edge of the work as possible—in the example below, it is just below the bind-off of a shoulder.

Working a backstitch seam

1 Pin the seam with right sides together. Bring the needle up through both first stitches, then back around the outside and up again through the same two stitches.

2 Take the needle back around the outside again, and bring it up one knitted stitch along the seam line.

3 Insert the needle where it last emerged, and bring it up again one more knitted stitch along the seam line. Repeat as required. Keep the stitches as even as possible.

349

All about yarn tails

Leave long tails at the beginning and end of a knitted piece—they will be useful later for joining seams. For intarsia (picture knitting) tails, see page 125. Otherwise, as you knit, or stitch seams, leave tails of at least 6in (15cm) and deal with them by one of the following methods.

Weaving in tails

Tails left from joining in or breaking off a color may be dealt with as you knit, by weaving them in on the wrong side in the same way as weaving floats in two-color knitting. Alternatively, on the next row, weave each tail over and under about ten stitches. After completion, pull gently to tighten the tail to match the stitch size, and snip off any excess.

Running in tails along a row

Thread the tail into a yarn needle and run it along the back of a row, up and down through the stitch loops, to match a woven-in tail.

Running in tails along a seam

Tails of 6in (15cm) or so may also be run in along a seam for about 2in (5cm), then snipped off short. Where two tails occur at the same point, run one tail up the seam, and the other down, to avoid excess bulk.

Running in slippery yarns

With slippery yarns, such as viscose, tails tend to slip out of place. Run them in for about 2in (5cm) and then back again in the opposite direction for a few stitches before snipping away the excess.

Crochet seams

Crochet makes a firm, ridged seam, often more suitable as a feature on the right side of the work. This seam is also sometimes used for shoulder seams instead of backstitch (page 142). For a neat finish, use a slightly finer yarn than that used for the knitting.

350 Working a single crochet seam for side edges

To join side edges of knitting, insert the crochet hook one stitch in from each edge. Try one crochet stitch per row. If the seam buckles, the number of stitches is too great, so try working two single crochet stitches together (page 139) at regular intervals.

351 Working a slip-stitch crochet seam

Working in slip stitch instead of single crochet, a very firm seam is produced but the edges of the knitting are not enclosed.

352 Working a single crochet seam for top or bottom edges

1 Hold the two pieces to be joined with right or wrong sides together, as desired. Insert the crochet hook through both edges together. On bound-off edges (as here), insert the hook through the centers of the stitches of the last row. (On cast-on edges, insert it between the stitches of the first row). Wrap the yarn and pull through a loop, leaving a tail of about 6in (15cm).

2 Hold the yarn tail along the back of the seam so that it is enclosed by the crochet stitches for the next 2in (5cm) or so: work in single crochet (page 138) through both edges together, matching the knitted stitches exactly together. When the seam is complete, cut the crochet yarn and run the tail under the crochet stitches with a yarn needle. Pull gently on the starting tail to settle it in place and snip off the excess. Other yarn tails left in the knitting may be enclosed in the same way as the starting crochet tail.

Binding off together

Two sets of stitches, equal in number, may be bound off together on the right side of the work to make a raised, decorative seam with a chain-stitch appearance. Or, make a slip bind-off seam (opposite), which is firm with minimal bulk on the wrong side of the work.

353 Binding off two edges together

1 If necessary, slip the stitches onto double-pointed needles so that both needles may be held together, with the wrong sides facing each other and with one of the yarn tails at the right. Insert a third needle knitwise through the first stitch on each needle and knit the two stitches together.

2 *Knit the next two stitches together in the same way; lift the first stitch on the third needle over the second stitch and off the needle. * Repeat from * to *, fastening off the last stitch in the usual way.

354

Making a slip bind-off seam

1 | Hold the two needles as in step 1 for binding off two edges together, but with the right sides facing each other. *Insert a third needle knitwise into the first stitch on the front needle, then purlwise into the first stitch on the back needle.

2 | Slip both stitches off onto the third needle. Use the back left-hand needle to lift the first stitch over the second stitch and off the third needle. *

3 | Repeat from * in step 1 to * in step 2, to the end of the row.

4 | Turn the work. Slip two stitches purlwise. ** Lift the first stitch over the second. Slip next stitch purlwise **. Repeat from ** to ** until one stitch remains. Pull one of the yarn tails left at the beginning of the first row through the last stitch to fasten it off.

5 | Now turn over your work to check the effect. The right side of the seam is very neat. This seam will not stretch out of shape.

FIX IT

355 *Yarn tail too short to run in?*

First pass the needle along the seam or through the backs of stitches, and then thread the tail into the needle eye. Pull through.

356 *Bulky yarn makes bulky seams?*

Bulky knits may be joined with ladder stitch, taking just one half of a stitch as a seam allowance on each edge instead of one whole stitch. The pieces should be knitted without selvage stitches. For heavily textured yarns, try a flat seam (page 142), using a finer yarn of matching color and fiber content.

357 *Seam too stretchy?*

Sometimes a seam needs to be firmed up for a neat fit that will not stretch, as on the shoulder of a sweater or vest. Use matching yarn to crochet a row of slip stitch along the wrong side of the seam.

Grafted seams

Use grafting to join two edges that have not been bound off. When worked correctly the seam is indistinguishable from a knitted row. There are no seam allowances, so there is no extra bulk to the seam. Use grafting where an ordinary seam might cause discomfort, for example on the toe of a sock. Grafting may also be used to make alterations without unraveling a complete piece, for example to shorten a sleeve.

Grafting is easier to work on simple stitches such as stockinette stitch and garter stitch because the yarn needle must follow the path of the stitches. Use a blunt-tipped yarn needle.

358

Grafting stockinette-stitch panels

You can graft two panels together provided that the stitches to be joined both run the same way and that they have the same number of stitches. Leave a long yarn tail at the end of each piece.

1 | Use a yarn needle to slip each set of stitches purlwise (page 57) onto a length of smooth, contrasting yarn (such as knitting cotton). Lay the two edges flat, with right sides uppermost, with one long yarn tail at upper right, threaded into the needle. (It doesn't matter where the other yarn tail is.)

2 | A contrasting thread (green) is used here for clarity but you should use your threaded yarn tail. Bring the needle up from the back through the center of the first stitch on the upper edge (knitwise). Now bring the needle up from the back, through the first stitch on the lower edge (purlwise).

3 | *Pull the yarn through gently. Pass the needle down through the center of the same upper stitch (purlwise), and up through the center of the next stitch (knitwise) in one movement.

4 | Pull the yarn through. Pass the needle down through the center of the same lower stitch (knitwise) and up through the center of the next stitch (purlwise)*.

5 | Repeat from * to * as required. Pull each stitch gently to match the size of the knitted stitches. When the seam is complete, run in both tails along the backs of the stitches, as page 143. If worked in matching yarn, this graft would look exactly like a row of knitting.

FIX IT

359 *Knitted piece is too long?*

If you've finished, for example, a sleeve and realize that the underarm length is too long, you don't have to unravel all the knitting. Choose a point where several rows can be removed, leaving the same number of stitches above and below. Snip a stitch at the center of the top row to be removed and unpick the row carefully, slipping the stitch loops of the row above purlwise onto a length of contrasting yarn. Unravel the unwanted rows plus one, and slip the stitches onto another length of yarn. Graft the two edges together.

360 *Finished piece too short?*

Snip a stitch at the center of a row and unpick the whole row, slipping the stitch loops of the row above onto a length of yarn. Pick up the loops of the row below onto a smaller needle, and then change to needles of correct size to work the extra rows you need. Graft the two edges together again.

361

Grafting garter-stitch panels

For a correct graft, one panel (shown as upper panel) must end with a right side row, and the other panel with a wrong side row.

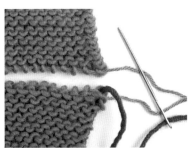

1 | Arrange the stitches as in step 1 for grafting stockinette-stitch panels. Thread the tail at upper right (from the piece ending a right-side row) into a yarn needle. A contrasting yarn (pink) is shown here for clarity, but you should use the yarn tail. Bring the needle up through the center of the first stitch on the lower edge from behind (purlwise), as shown.

4 | Pass the needle up through the center of the same upper stitch (knitwise). * Repeat from * in step 2 to *. Finish as for grafting stockinette-stitch panels, step 5. The grafted row duplicates the appearance of a row of garter stitch.

2 | Bring needle up through the center of the first upper stitch (knitwise). * Pull the yarn through. Take the needle down through the center of the next upper stitch (purlwise). Pull the yarn through.

3 | Pass the needle down through the center of the same lower stitch (knitwise) and up through the center of the next stitch (purlwise). Pull the yarn through.

⊚TRY IT

362 **Try before you join**

Baste seams on a garment and check it for size before assembly. That way if the fit needs adjustment, you can do something about it now. Baste with a strong, smooth yarn in a contrast color (sewing thread is not strong enough), taking the needle up and down through the work to make simple basting stitches about ½in (12mm) long that will be easy to remove after completion.

⊚TRY IT

363 **Grafting from needles**

Once you understand how the grafted yarn follows the path of a knitted row, you may prefer to graft directly from the knitting needles, although this method can make it more difficult to match the gauge of the knitted stitches. You may need to slip the stitches purlwise (page 57) onto double-pointed needles to arrange them in the same positions as for grafting stockinette-stitch panels. Follow the instructions for grafting, inserting the yarn needle knitwise or purlwise through each stitch, and allowing the grafted stitches to drop from the needles as work progresses.

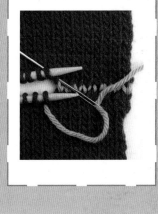

Pressing and blocking

No matter how neatly you knit or how experienced you are, your knitted items will still look better if they are pressed and/or blocked. These procedures even out any stitch irregularities, uncurl your pieces, and leave them looking professionally knitted. Pressing or blocking before assembly also makes it easier to produce neat seams.

364 Tips for pressing and blocking

• Consult the ball band(s) to find out if yarns may be pressed, and if so, at what temperature. If not, use the blocking method. As a rule of thumb, natural-fiber yarns such as wool and cotton may be pressed. Synthetic yarns and blends, and many textured yarns, are best treated by blocking.
• Boldly textured stitches in any yarn may be flattened and spoiled by pressing so use the blocking method instead.

365 Pressing

Correct pressing will help even out the stitches and "set" the shape, but refer to the tips above and do not press your knitted pieces unless you are sure it is safe to do so.

Pressing before assembly

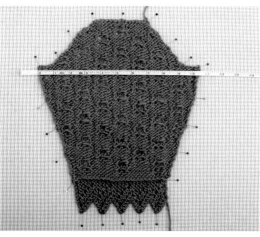

1 | Pin the knitting right side down on a blocking board (see opposite), flat and square. (Small pieces may be pinned out on an ironing board.) Check the measurements as you pin. Use large-headed pins at right angles to the edges, about 1–2in (2.5–5cm) apart, all around the edge of the work.

2 | Heat the iron to the recommended temperature. Some ball bands recommend pressing under a dry cloth; others under a damp cloth or using steam. If steam is required, wring out a clean cotton cloth in cold water until it is just damp (not wet). Whether steaming or not, lay the cloth over the work and rest the iron gently on the surface. Do not press down hard. Do not move the iron around on the surface, but lift and replace it to treat the whole area. Avoid pressing ribbed borders as this will make them less elastic. Remove the cloth and leave the work to cool and/or dry completely before unpinning it.

Pressing after assembly

Assuming that you have already pressed the individual pieces, all you need to work on now are the seams. Press them lightly on the wrong side in the same way as above.

366
Blocking

Always use this technique for yarns labeled "do not press." It is also suitable for "cool iron only" yarns, highly textured or fluffy yarns, boldly textured stitch patterns, and items such as circular-knit hats which cannot easily be laid flat.

Blocking before assembly

1 Wash the knitting gently by hand in lukewarm water using suitable detergent. Squeeze gently; do not rub. To avoid stretching the knitting, do not lift it out, but drain away the water. Do not wring. Rinse in three changes of lukewarm water.

2 Roll the knitting in a towel to blot away excess moisture. Never use a spin or tumble dryer unless you actively wish to felt the knitting.

3 Pin the knitting on a blocking board (see below) in the same way as for pressing and leave the board flat until the work is completely dry.

Blocking after assembly

Awkward shapes such as this sock may be dried on a "former" cut to shape from stout cardboard (or you can buy wooden versions if you make a lot of socks). Add a hanging loop, as shown, to hang the knitting in a warm, airy place away from direct sunlight.

A three-dimensional knit, like this circular-knit hat, may be dried on a suitable "former," such as this plastic tub.

A completed garment can be blocked in the same way as above and dried flat on a towel, patting it gently to shape. This intarsia sweater combines smooth wool/ synthetic yarn for the blue background with white fuzzy yarn for the dog, so blocking is the best way to finish it without affecting the contrasting textures.

367
Don't know which method to use?

If you have lost the ball band and don't know how to finish your knitting, use your gauge sample for a test piece. Press or block it as you think appropriate before treating the finished project.

368
Making a blocking board

A special board is useful for pinning out large pieces. About 24 x 36in (60 x 90cm) is a useful size. Cover a piece of plywood with a layer of batting, then a top layer of cotton fabric, folded over the edges and stapled to the back. Gingham fabric will provide an instant grid for pinning straight edges.

Aftercare

Take time to clean your knitted items properly—after all, you've taken the time to knit them. Look after them carefully and they will last for years, even decades. Different fibers require different treatments: nowadays, ball bands should carry all the necessary information you need.

369 Aftercare tips

• Save a ball band from each yarn used in a project for future reference, or sew care labels into your garments. Printed care labels may be obtained in bulk, or use a laundry marker and white labeling tape to write your own.
• If an item is stained, spot-treat the stain before washing.
• If in doubt about the best method to use, test any process on a gauge swatch that includes all the yarns used for a project.

• If an item needs repairing, do this before washing or dry-cleaning. To be prepared for future repairs, keep a small ball of each yarn and wash it in a net laundry bag each time you wash the item, so the colors will always match.
• Fasten all buttons or other fastenings. Pocket openings and front bands may also be basted closed so they cannot stretch out of shape during washing.

International care symbols
The symbols may be found on ball bands.

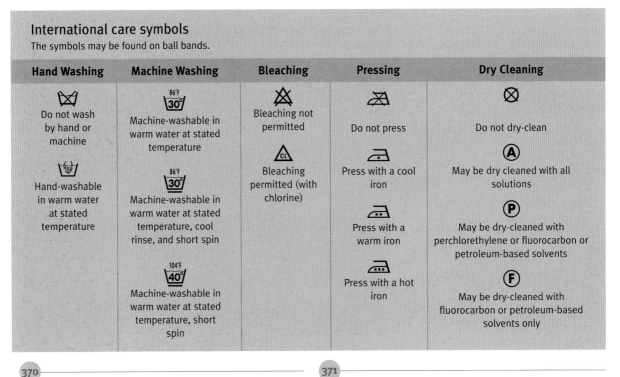

Hand Washing	Machine Washing	Bleaching	Pressing	Dry Cleaning
Do not wash by hand or machine	86°F 30° Machine-washable in warm water at stated temperature	Bleaching not permitted	Do not press	Do not dry-clean
Hand-washable in warm water at stated temperature	86°F 30° Machine-washable in warm water at stated temperature, cool rinse, and short spin	cl Bleaching permitted (with chlorine)	Press with a cool iron	(A) May be dry cleaned with all solutions
	104°F 40° Machine-washable in warm water at stated temperature, short spin		Press with a warm iron	(P) May be dry-cleaned with perchlorethylene or fluorocarbon or petroleum-based solvents
			Press with a hot iron	(F) May be dry-cleaned with fluorocarbon or petroleum-based solvents only

370 Hand washing

Wash and rinse the work in the same way as for blocking, and lay it flat on a towel or a mesh drying screen. Pat the garment out to match the original measurements. A three-dimensional shape may be dried on a "former," as for blocking. Leave to dry completely. Turning the garment over before it is completely dry will speed the drying process.

When dry, the item may be lightly pressed, as page 148. Always consult the care instructions on the ball band(s) for the correct temperature setting.

371 Machine washing

Many modern yarns are now labeled "machine-washable" or "superwash." The ball band should tell you the maximum machine temperature to use. Dry as for hand washing unless the label specifies that the yarn may be machine-dried.

Dry-cleaning

Most modern yarns may also be dry-cleaned. Take care to remove any trims, such as buttons or ribbons if these are not dry-cleanable. After cleaning, remove any plastic wrapping, and hang the garment for a few hours in a well-ventilated place, away from direct sunlight: use a mesh drying screen, or a padded coat-hanger, or lay the garment over a solid rod (not a washing line) and turn it once or twice.

373

Storing knitwear

Fold and store your knitwear correctly to avoid creasing, losing shape, and fading.
• Always wash or clean as above before storing.
• Never hang knitted garments on coat hangers or they will drop out of shape.
• Keep folded knits away from heat, damp, dust, and direct sunlight. A drawer or chest is ideal.
• Do not squash the folded knits, though they may be loosely stacked.
• Natural animal fibers such as wool and mohair attract moths, so you may wish to use moth prevention. Cotton fibers and synthetics do not attract moths.
• For long-term storage, place tissue paper on top of the unfolded garment and fold as shown below. Loosely wrap each sweater with more tissue paper to allow air to circulate.

FIX IT

374 *Fluffy yarn looks flat after washing?*

Garments made from mohair yarns and similar blends may be lightly brushed with a teasel brush (page 12) to raise the pile and restore the fluffy appearance. Angora garments will fluff up again after a couple of hours in a plastic bag placed in the freezer.

Folding a basic sweater or jacket

Use this folding method for light- to medium-weight garments. Jackets may be folded in the same way after fastening the fronts together.

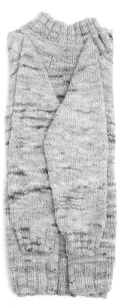

2 | Fold the lower edge up to meet the shoulder line. Turn over.

1 | Lay the sweater front side down on a flat surface. Fold one sleeve and one-quarter of the front toward the back so the side seam is at center back. Fold the sleeve downwards. Fold the other half of the sweater in the same way.

Folding a bulky sweater

Use this method for bulky sweaters, drop-shoulder shapes, and straight armhole shapes.

1 | Lay the sweater front side down on a flat surface. Fold back each sleeve in line with the side seam.

2 | Fold the lower edge up to meet the shoulder line. Turn over.

Glossary

3-ply, 4-ply: light-weight knitting yarns, sometimes called fingering.

acrylic: a synthetic fiber.

Angora: very soft yarn fiber made from the combed fur of the Angora rabbit, usually blended with other fibers.

Aran-weight: a medium- to heavy-weight yarn.

backstitch: a firm sewing stitch, also used to embroider fine lines and outlines.

bamboo: fiber from the bamboo plant, used to make a smooth, silky yarn; also the woody stem, used to make knitting needles.

batwing: a garment shape, normally with sleeves and body knitted all in one piece.

binding off: fastening off stitches so they will not unravel.

block, blocking: treating a piece of knitting (by washing and/or pressing) to set its shape.

bobbin: a plastic or cardboard holder for a small amount of yarn.

bouclé yarn: a fancy yarn with a knobbly effect.

bulky: a heavy-weight yarn, sometimes called chunky.

button band or button border: a separate band, knitted sideways or lengthwise, to which buttons are sewn.

buttonhole band or buttonhole border: a separate band, knitted sideways or lengthwise, with buttonholes worked as knitting proceeds.

cable needle: a small double-pointed needle used to work cables.

cable: the crossing of two groups of stitches.

casting on: making new stitches on a needle.

chain stitch: an embroidery stitch, used for medium-width, curved lines.

chenille: a type of yarn that makes a velvety texture when knitted.

chevron: a knitted zigzag formation made by increasing and decreasing.

chunky: a heavy-weight yarn, sometimes called bulky.

circular knitting: worked with a circular needle, or a set of double-pointed needles, to form a tube.

collar stand: extra short rows worked above a

neckline, but below a collar, to improve fit.

cotton: a natural fiber from the cotton plant.

counted-stitch embroidery: worked by stitching over knitted stitches, following a chart.

crew (neck): a round, close-fitting neckline.

cross stitch: a stitch used for counted-stitch embroidery.

cuff: the lower border of a sleeve.

decreasing: working stitches together to reduce their number.

double knitting: a medium-weight yarn.

double-pointed needle: a knitting needle with a point at each end.

drape: the feel of yarn or knitting, and how it behaves in use.

drop shoulder: formed by a sleeve with a straight top edge, joined to a garment body with no armhole shapings.

duplicate stitch: an embroidery stitch that copies knitted stitches, also known as Swiss darning or kitchener stitch.

dye-lot number: indicates exact dye bath used, not just shade.

ease: the difference between body measurement and actual garment measurement

Fair Isle knitting: small repeating patterns, knitted with two or more colors.

felting needle: used to embellish with yarns.

felting: the process of shrinking knitting to make a firm fabric.

fingering: a fine weight yarn (similar to 3-ply and 4-ply).

flat seam: a method of joining knitted pieces.

float: the strand of yarn left at the wrong side of the work when stranding.

freestyle embroidery: worked by following a drawn or traced outline.

French knot: an embroidery stitch forming a small rounded knot.

fully-fashioned shaping: shaping emphasized by working decreases (or increases) two or more stitches in from the edge of the work.

garter stitch: formed by working all stitches as knit on every row.

gauge: the number of stitches and rows to a given measurement.

grafting: a seamless method of joining knitted pieces.

hank: a coil of yarn.

I-cord: (idiot cord) a tubular knitted cord made with two double-pointed needles.

increasing: making extra stitches.

intarsia: another name for picture knitting.

invisible seam: a seam stitched with ladder stitch.

knitwise: as when knitting a stitch.

ladder stitch: (also known as mattress stitch, or invisible seam) a neat method of joining knitted pieces.

lazy daisy: another name for single chain stitch.

linen: a natural fiber derived from the flax plant

lurex: a metallic fiber used to make yarn, either alone or blended with other fibers.

mattress stitch: another name for ladder stitch.

medallion: a unit for knitted patchwork: square, round, hexagonal (or other regular shape).

metallic: yarn or fiber with a metallic effect.

miter: a shaped corner formed on a border.

mohair: a natural fiber, hair from the Angora goat.

mosaic knitting: repeating patterns in two or more colors, knitted using one color at a time by means of slip stitches.

natural fiber: fiber naturally occurring as an animal or vegetable product.

needle gauge: a small gadget for checking the size of knitting needles.

pattern: a stitch pattern, or a set of instructions for making a garment.

pearl cotton: a slightly glossy embroidery thread suitable for use on knitting.

picot: a little nub formed with knit or crochet stitches, normally repeated along an edging.

polo (neck): a round neckline with buttons at center front, often with a collar.

polyamide: a synthetic fiber.

polyester: a synthetic fiber.

purlwise: as when purling a stitch.

raglan: a sleeve and armhole shaping that slopes from the armhole to the neck edge.

ramie: fiber from the ramie plant, used to make a smooth yarn.

reverse stockinette stitch: stockinette stitch worked with the purl side as the right side.

rib stitches or ribbing: various combinations of knit and purl stitches, arranged to form vertical lines.

ribbon yarn: a fancy yarn, made from flat tape.

right and left (when describing parts of a garment): describe where the garment part will be when worn, e.g. the right sleeve is worn on the right arm.

right side: the side of the work that will be outside the garment when worn.

ring marker: a smooth unbroken ring of metal or plastic, slipped onto a needle to mark a particular position along a row, and slipped from row to row as knitting proceeds.

seam: the join made when two pieces of knitting are sewn together.

seed stitch: a stitch pattern with a "dotted" appearance.

selvage stitch: the first or last stitch(es) of a row worked in a different way to the rest of the row, to make a decorative edge, or a firm, neat edge for seaming.

set-in sleeve: a sleeve and armhole shaping where the armhole is curved to take a curved sleeve head.

shank: a pierced stem on the back of a button, used for attaching it; also a similar stem made with sewing thread.

shaping: increasing or decreasing the number of stitches to form the shape required.

shawl (collar): a large collar that wraps the neck like a shawl.

Shetland wool: loosely-spun sheepswool from the Shetland Islands.

short-row shaping: the process of working incomplete rows to shape the knitting.

silk: a natural fiber from the cocoon of the silkworm.

single chain stitch: an embroidery stitch used for flower petals, etc.

skein: a loosely-wound coil of yarn or embroidery thread.

slip stitch: a stitch slipped from one needle to the other without working into it.

slub yarn or slubby yarn: yarn of uneven thickness.

soft cotton: a heavy-weight embroidery thread suitable for use on knitting.

sport-weight: a medium-weight yarn.

stem stitch: a freestyle embroidery stitch.

stitch holder: a device for holding stitches temporarily.

stitch marker: a split ring of metal or plastic, slipped onto a knitted stitch to mark a position.

stockinette stitch: formed by working one row of knit stitches, one row of purl stitches, and repeating these two rows.

stranding: a method of dealing with floats in two-color knitting.

Swiss darning: another term for duplicate stitch.

synthetic fiber: manufactured fiber, not naturally occurring.

tapestry needle: a sewing needle with a blunt tip and a large eye.

tapestry wool: wool sold in small skeins for embroidery.

teasel brush: a small, stiff brush.

tweed yarn: yarn spun with flecks of contrasting colors, to resemble tweed fabric.

twisting: a method of dealing with floats in two-color knitting.

viscose rayon: a man-made fiber derived from cellulose.

weaving: a method of dealing with floats in two-color knitting.

wool: a natural fiber from the coat of sheep.

worsted: a medium-weight yarn.

wrong side: the side of the work that will be inside the garment when worn.

yoke: the neck and shoulder area of a garment, esp. where this is made all in one piece.

Common abbreviations

Always read the list of abbreviations used in any knitting pattern. Different suppliers may use different abbreviations, and they may be upper- or lower-case letters. Here are some of the most commonly used abbreviations:

alt	alternate
approx	approximately
B	bobble or bead
BC	back cross; back cable
beg	beginning
bet	between
BH	buttonhole
BO	bind off
C	cable; cross
CC	contrast color
ch	chain
col	color
cm(s)	centimeter(s)
cn	cable needle
CO	cast on
cont	continue
dc	double crochet
dec(s)	decrease(s), decreasing
DK	double knitting
dpn	double pointed needle(s)
EOR	every other row or round
ER	every row or round
est	established
FC	front cross; front cable
foll	follow(ing)
g, gr, or gm	gram
grp(s)	group(s)
g st	garter stitch
hk	(crochet) hook
in(s)	inch(es)
inc(s)	increase(s), increasing
incl	include, including
K; k	knit
Kb; K1b	knit stitch in row below, or knit stitch through back loop
Kbf	knit into back and front of same stitch
Kfb	knit into front and back of same stitch
K2tog	knit 2 together
Kwise	knitwise
LC	left cross; left cable
LH	left hand
lp(s)	loop(s)
LT	left twist
M	marker
m	meter(s)
MB	make bobble
MC	main color
meas	measure(s)
mm	millimeter(s)
m1	make one

m1tbl or m1b	make one through back loop; invisible increase
ndl	needle
no	number
oz	ounce
P; p	purl
pat; patt	pattern
Pb; P1b	purl stitch in row below; or purl stitch through back loop
Pbf	purl into back and front of same stitch
Pfb	purl into front and back of same stitch
pm	place marker
pnso	pass next stitch over
psso	pass slip stitch over
Ptbl	purl through back loop
P2tog	purl 2 together
Pwise	purlwise
RC	right cross; right cable
rem	remaining
rep	repeat
rev st st	reverse stockinette stitch
RH	right hand
rib	ribbing
rd(s) or rnd(s)	round(s)
RS	right side (of work)
RT	right twist
sc	single crochet
sk	skip
SKP, skpo	slip 1, knit 1, pass slip stitch over
sl	slip
sl st	slip stitch
sM	slip marker
sp(s)	space(s)
ssk	slip, slip, knit
st(s)	stitch(es)
st st	stockinette stitch
s2togpo	vertical double decrease
tbl	through back loop(s)
tch	turning chain
tog	together
tr	treble
WS	wrong side (of work)
wyib	with yarn in back, as if to knit
wyif	with yarn in front, as if to purl
yb or ybk	yarn to the back between needles
yd	yard
yf or yfwd	yarn to the front between needles
yo or yon	yarn over needle to make extra stitch
yrn	yarn round needle to make extra stitch

Common symbols

Always read the list of symbols given in the key to any chart. Patterns from different sources may use different symbols. Some symbols are worked differently depending on whether they fall on a right-side row (RS) or a wrong-side row (WS), see page 23.

✚	selvage stitch
▯ or ▯	stockinette stitch — RS: K, WS: P
▬ or •	reverse stockinette stitch — RS: P, WS: K
⅊ or ⁄	twisted stockinette stitch — RS: Ktbl; WS: Ptbl
V	slip stitch knitwise
V or ▯	slip stitch purlwise
O	yarn over
⅄ or U	make one through back loop
⋎ or V	increase 1 stitch - RS: knit into front and back of stitch; WS: purl into back and front of stitch
▼	(k1, p1, k1) all in same stitch
V or ▼	multiple increase (refer to key)
⋌ or ◹	right-slanting decrease — RS: K2tog; WS: P2tog
⋋ or ◸	left-slanting decrease — RS: Ssk; WS: P2tog tbl
⋌ or ◢	right-slanting double decrease — RS: K3tog; WS: P3tog

⋋ or ◣	left-slanting double decrease — RS: sl1, K2tog, psso; WS: sl2tog, sl1k, sl 3 sts back to LH ndl and P3togtbl
⋀	vertical double decrease – RS: sl2tog, K1, psso
⋀ or ▲	multiple decrease (refer to key)
▬	bind off
■	no stitch
• or ◉	knot or bobble (refer to key)
⋈ or ⟋	right twist (2 sts)
⋈ or ⟍	left twist (2 sts)

larger twists and cables may be shown in various ways, e.g.:

⋈⋈ or ⟋⟋	cable 4 sts to right
⋈⋈⋈ or ⋈⋈	cable 6 sts to left

Crochet hook sizes

US steel hooks	US aluminum/ plastic hooks	International metric sizes (all hooks)
14	—	0.6mm
13	—	0.75mm
12	—	1mm
11	—	—
10	—	1.25mm
9	—	—
8	—	1.5mm
7	—	—
6	—	1.75mm
5	—	—
4	—	2mm
3	—	—
2	B	2.25mm
1	C	2.5mm
0	D	3mm
00	E	3.5mm
—	F	—
—	—	4mm
—	G	—
—	—	4.5mm
—	H	5mm
—	I	5.5mm
—	J	6mm
—	K	6.5mm
—	L	7mm
—	M	8mm
—	N	9mm
—	—	10mm
—	—	12mm
—	—	15mm

Use the chart above to switch between US and metric sizes.

Index

Figures in italics indicate captions; those in bold type indicate main references.

Common abbreviations

Fold-out this flap while you work though the book for an at-a-glance reminder of the most commonly used abbreviations.

Credits

Author's acknowledgments
The author would like to thank Brown Sheep Co. Inc.,
Debbie Bliss, and Twilleys for supplying yarns featured in
the book, and also the hand models, Julie Joubinaux and
Emily Mattinson.

Quarto would like to thank the following knitters,
agencies and manufacturers for supplying images for
inclusion in this book:

The DMC Corporation, www.dmc-usa.com, pp.18-19
Nibbs, Jo, www.etsy.com/uk/shop/craftyjoes, p.29
Rowan, www.knitrowan.com, pp.4, 28, 32, 60cr, 65bl , 68,
70, 71, 75, 79tr, 117tl